It is not every day that one comes across a book that combines literary style, theological insight, and an unsentimental encounter with hard realities of the city. In fact, it has been a very long time since I have read anything like *Voices from the City*. This is bracing stuff—and not only for those who are in urban ministry.

(The Rev.) Richard John Neuhaus
President, Religion and Public Life

Nunes clearly understands that what the city needs is biblical theology. Urban residents experience the various deaths of the Law daily; this book urges preachers to name it and celebrate the victory of the Gospel over it. Good instruction for all of us who care about the people in the city!

Marva J. Dawn
Adjunct Professor of Spiritual Theology
Regent College, Vancouver, BC
Member, Lutheran Inner-City Ministries
Portland, OR

Even the casual reader will detect Nunes' passion for the city and his understanding of its ills, its racism, its unemployment and inadequate education. But Nunes goes beyond description; he shows how to apply the core values of Lutheranism—Law and Gospel, Word and Sacrament, justification and sanctification—to the urban scene. Pastors and laypersons with roots in other Christian traditions will appreciate the issues and images Nunes identifies and the solution he puts forward: the Christ who has experienced human anguish and suffering who is for us and with us in His Gospel victory!

(The Rev.) William Griffin
Area Representative, Wheat Ridge Ministries

Voices from the City

Voices from the City

Issues and Images of Urban Preaching

John Nunes

SAINT LOUIS

Excerpts from *Christ and Culture* and *Concordia Journal* used by permission of Concordia Seminary Publications.

Excerpts from the *Book of Concord* ed. by Theodore G. Tappert, Copyright ©1983 Fortress Press. Used with permission.

Excerpt from "The Myth of Community Development" by Nicholas Lemann reprinted by permission of International Creative Management, Inc. Copyright ©1994 Nicholas Lemann.

Excerpt from *Jesus through the Centuries* by Jaroslav Pelikan reprinted by permission of Yale University Press. Copyright ©1985 Yale University.

Excerpt from *Loose Canons: Notes on the Culture Wars* by Henry Louis Gates Jr. reprinted by permission of Oxford University Press. Copyright ©1992 Henry Louis Gates Jr.

Scripture quotations taken from the HOLY BIBLE, NEW INTERNATIONAL VERSION®. NIV®. Copyright © 1973, 1978, 1984 by International Bible Society. Used by permission of Zondervan Publishing House. All rights reserved.

To Monique and my family

Contents

Foreword

During the 1960s and 1970s, much mainline and evangelical denominational literature on urban ministry was skewed in two seemingly contradictory yet mutually distorting ways. First, there were books that used the term "urban ministry" as a euphemism for ministry among poor blacks and Latinos, thereby minimizing the metropolitan character of ministry in the city and its environs. Second, there were texts that glorified and emphasized the contributions of those who had "come back" to the city as missionaries, thereby rendering silent the voices of those who had remained faithful during the time of urban flight.

John Nunes' text offers correctives to both viewpoints. He sees the systemic context of ministry in the city, focusing his attention on churches and institutions in a variety of venues within the metropolitan areas of our country. He hears the voices of those who have remained faithful in those places, enduring the changes, abandonment, promises, joys, and frustrations of all that is life in the metropolis.

Nunes shows us ministry that is responsive to the simple call to follow Christ among the poor. He reveals the reality of the complexity of the systems and institutions in which we are called to be faithful. By focusing on the preached word and enabling us to hear the voices of God's preachers, Nunes resists the reductionist tendencies of many urban ministry texts and offers a rich landscape of metropolitan possibilities for the church of Christ.

Rev. Harold Dean Trulear, Ph.D.
Vice President, Director of Church Collaboration Initiatives
Public/Private Ventures

Introduction

Issues and images. The issues are complex. The debate is often heated. The points of contention are as concrete as life and death. Likewise, the images are hard-core. Crime, poverty, diversity, and opportunity whiz by at a breakneck tempo.

Christian ministry in the city presents unique issues and images. Amid this flux, the message of the Gospel is constant. It is a message in continuity with the prophets of old, except these voices are crying out in an urban wilderness.

Urban preachers are prayerful prophets and poets who speak God's saving story in Jesus Christ within the primary liturgical context of Word and Sacrament. That sacred arena for speaking includes all the places where people work, sleep, play, and pray. Here, the Word spoken and heard becomes enfleshed in life.

The genre of this book bears similarity to the nonfiction memoirist-reportage style, what Joyce Carol Oates refers to as a "hybrid" of research, interviews, analysis, and personal perspective.[1]

The intent of this book is to document the living, ongoing drama of communicating the Gospel on the street-level stage of the city. The players are God's own: preachers who strive to maintain a Lutheran identity on the raw edges—indeed, the bleeding edges—of American urban life. Similarly, those who hear that sacred story are God's own people; redeemed sinners/saints are the object of this drama. God is always the Subject, the Actor, the Principal, and the Agent of salvation. The story of his promise intersects the human story from beginning to end, a story full of grace and truth (John 1:14).

A primary feature of the following pages is interviews with ministers on the front lines. These pastors possess a contagious passion for the Word and an excitement for proclaiming it to people. The singularity of their commitment is exemplary. The scope of their sincerity shines through even amid the gargantuan challenges they face. It comes through in a commitment to maintain integrity to Christ's call to ministry despite adversity. It comes through in a compassion for people in pain. It comes through in a devotion to proclaim the promises of God made known in the benefits of Christ "even when steeples are falling." It comes, in some cases, even as neglect and a persistent lack of resources ravage their cavernous church buildings. But these ministers preach on.

They preach because at the core of their conviction is victory in Jesus. These pastors are Gospel preachers. With words and images, they draw straight lines of connection between the Good News of universal victory and the pervasive and perverse experiences of urban defeat. The voices represented in this volume have been chosen deliberately because of their depth of reflection on urban ministry questions. Quite incidentally they also represent a range of people groups found in the city. They serve black, white, Hispanic, and Asian families and communities. These communities are places of diverse social and ethnic strata.

The interviews for this book were conducted March 11–13, 1996. At that time, the interviewees were serving in the following places of ministry:

The Rev. Donald E. Anthony, pastor,
Berea Lutheran Church (LCMS),
Baltimore, Maryland

The Rev. Victor J. Belton, pastor,
Peace Lutheran Church (LCMS),
Decatur (Atlanta), Georgia

The Rev. Dr. James Capers, pastor,
St. Paul Lutheran Church (ELCA),
Decatur (Atlanta), Georgia

The Rev. John R. Cochran, pastor,
Trinity Lutheran Church (ELCA),
Pittsburgh, Pennsylvania

The Rev. Joseph Donnella, Lutheran chaplain
(ELCA), Howard University,
Washington, D.C.

The Rev. Carlos Hernandez, pastor,
Trinity Lutheran Church (LCMS),
Glen Cove (Long Island), New York

The Rev. Steven Marsh, pastor,
St. Luke's Lutheran Church (ELCA),
Brooklyn, New York

The Rev. Ulmer Marshall, pastor,
Trinity Lutheran Church (LCMS),
Mobile, Alabama

The Rev. Dr. Frazier N. Odom, pastor,
Transfiguration Lutheran Church (LCMS),
Saint Louis, Missouri

The Rev. Doyle J. Theimer, pastor,
Saint John the Evangelist (LCMS),
Brooklyn, New York

The Rev. James Wetzstein, pastor,
Our Savior Lutheran Church (LCMS),
Gary, Indiana

What Is Urban?

The voices are many. From trained experts to amateur demographers, opinions abound on what defines "urban." For some, "urban" is merely a euphemism: a kinder and gentler way to say Asian, black, Hispanic, or any other concentration of non-middle-class Anglo people. From this perspective, "urban" is any ghetto inhabited by socioethnic groups other than the majority population. Others look at the term "urban" more expansively. They use it to describe the geographical links among suburbs, inner-ring suburbs, inner-city, and ex-urban communities.

Urban *ministry* is most often understood as a set of complex cultural and demographic conditions that require specialized spiritual gifts. An urban ministry setting is more like a non-Western mission setting than a traditional parish-based ministry. It is, however, important to distinguish between doing urban ministry and doing ministry in an urban setting. Urban ministry requires a high degree of sensitivity to the context. It requires a theologizing that correlates to the community.

> Brooklyn, New York, is unquestionably urban.
> There are a lot of immigrants. New York is one of the
> most political places I have ever been. [It has] a lot of
> activism for that reason and a lot of sensitivity to
> racial issues.—Doyle J. Theimer

Even some comfortably suburban communities—once looked on as "distant" suburbs—are taking on the flavor of urban life, as well as the benefits and the costs. Few communities could better typify the suburbs and the flight from the central cities than postwar Long Island. Levittown was basically Suburbia, U.S.A., yet many or most portions of Long Island are now urban.

> Long Island, New York, ... has more features of an
> urban community than it does of a suburban. It has
> HUD housing. Some of it is almost like being in
> Queens.—Carlos Hernandez

So-called "inner-ring" suburbs can be extremely urban. These suburbs are the geopolitical units closest to the city, like Prince George's County, Maryland (Washington, D.C.); Melrose Park, Illinois (Chicago); or Southfield, Michigan (Detroit). Often, these suburbs date back to the early 20th century and represent some of the oldest growth rings beyond the city limits. Sometimes they suffer from the same crumbling infrastructures afflicting the core city.

Is any place immune to urban problems? Some argue that access to electronic communication and the ready availability of five hundred cable channels has created a global *city*, in contrast to a global *village*. Supporters of this view contend that even remote crossroads in our postmodern world now have urban features. This drives home the imperative of studying the cities and of developing a theology that is appropriate for the city. Preaching, as the place where the theological rubber of the pulpits hits the pew of human experience, is a good place to begin.

Place of Paradox

The paradoxical notions of Lutheran theology, I think are most revealing and helpful for an urban context. We often talk about threat and promise— about Law and Gospel—in classical Lutheran language. But we could also extend that paradoxical language in other ways. We can help urban people to understand that not only do threat and promise characterize our relationship with God, but threat and promise characterize life in our cities. The promise, of course, is God's transforming grace and love among people.—Joseph Donnella

Paradoxes are built into the reality of life. Arguably, these paradoxes are more pronounced and more profoundly encountered in urban areas. The marginal edges of life can be sharper in the city. The sinner in us is easy to nourish with the ample availability of temptation. The saint, by contrast, can approach the heroic because of ample opportunities for expressing faith through service to God and neighbor. An example of this paradox is conveyed in the fact that blacks living in the United States are often the most religiously conservative and evangelically traditional people on the planet. In fact, inner cities have many more pew spaces per capita than suburban communities. On the other hand, the paradox persists: genuine piety alongside indulgent pathology.

Law and Gospel are very important. Young people, young people, and young people surround us all the time. It isn't just talking about forgiveness, but there are many applications of the Law, which Luther didn't

*think about. It is the measured balance, balance, bal-
ance of the Law and the Gospel for living; the Law
and the Gospel, spoken over and over, in every situation, is very, very, very important.—John R.
Cochran*

In the final analysis, what urban believers share in common—
their struggles and their celebrations—supersedes their social and
ethnic differences. Each believer experiences the challenge of keeping faith in that uniquely modern geopolitical unit, the large city.
In each of these voices from the city, there is a pastoral passion for
getting the Gospel into the hearts and lives of God's people.
Finally, and not to be overlooked, we hear in each voice a commitment to theologize in a manner consistent with Lutheran identity.
That truth is nonnegotiable. (God's truth is revealed in the Old
and New Testaments, a truth that has been entrusted to the
Confessional writings of the Lutheran church. These writings clearly flow from the Bible, the "pure and clear fountain" of God's
Word.) What does vary, and greatly at times, is the context in which
that one truth is spoken.

*We did a vacation Bible school and I renamed [it]
"Our VBS," [which stood for] "Values, Beauty, and
Strength" ... Our Lutheran doctrine and the Bible in
particular teach that we are valuable people. If that
was not the case, Christ would not have come and
died for us no matter our situation of life. We are
beautiful people because we are created in the image
of God. We are strong people because we have the
strength of God. The strength of Christ who overcame
death and everything else is at our disposal. In our
church, we teach [that all of this is] a gift ... a free
gift that you don't have to work for ... It's God's gift,
and I think that is a tremendous message for people*

who feel like they cannot do any better; who feel like they are trapped; people who don't have a good image of themselves because of their surroundings, because of what they see every day, because of what they hear every day. I believe the Gospel really frees us up to say that no matter what we think about ourselves at the moment, Christ thinks a whole lot of us. He enables us to think better of ourselves because of what he has done. That's a gift that we just simply receive. It has a tremendous freeing power. That's the Gospel; it's what we teach in the Lutheran church.—Donald E. Anthony

While serving in Detroit, I received an urgent phone call from a pastor in a difficult ministry situation. He needed advice on a question usually associated with urban settings. But he was not calling from L.A. or D.C. His home was the Midwest, but not the major metropolitan centers of St. Louis or Kansas City. The request came from a pastor in Missouri serving in a city that does not even rank among the top 20 metropolitan areas in the state. He wanted my help as he counseled a family in crisis. The teenage son, recently confirmed in the faith of Christ, was running for his life—literally. He was caught up in gang crossfire between rival Bloods and Cripts. The pastor wanted fast, reliable information for his ministry and community: How should I intervene? What do I say to the family? to my congregation? He was dealing with big city problems in small-town Middle America!

Both an Evangelical Lutheran Church in America (Dr. James Capers) and a Lutheran Church—Missouri Synod (Rev. Victor Belton) congregation in suburban Atlanta are represented in these interviews. The setting for both congregations (Decatur, Georgia) unquestionably qualifies them as "urban." In these churches, three distinct characteristics emerge that serve to define the ministry setting as urban: poverty, violent crime, and diversity.

The variety that exists demographically in the met-
ropolitan [Atlanta] area is the variety that exists
here at Peace Lutheran Church. At any one time, we
are speaking to Boomers and Busters and Generation
Xers and war generation folks. They all have a pref-
erence for how they would like to hear the Lord pre-
sented.—Victor J. Belton

Inescapable Realities

What ails cities is not hard to detect. The symptoms are easily discernable. Too much of what we see and hear of urban life is
defeat:

- Streets strewn with broken glass.

- Streets lined with a surplus of liquor stores.

- Streets dotted with stores suffering from a famine
  of necessities such as fresh milk and bread without
  mold.

- Streets as backdrops for defeated existences eked
  out in crumbling buildings tagged with the script of
  gang machismo, hieroglyphics of hate that boastful-
  ly promise death to rivals.

- Streets populated by preadolescent boys, who are
  too young to be so radically alienated from human
  values, yet are lifelessly living defeated existences.

To all appearances, it is defeat when children unconscionably
commit murder for something as insignificant as an article of clothing or something as intangible as honor. It is defeat when young
boys, not yet men, die prematurely, holding guns too big for their
not fully formed hands. It is defeat when pubescent girls, living
prematurely in grown women's bodies, give birth to inheritors of
multigenerational poverty and dependency. It is defeat when those

who rightly draw our greatest sympathy, defeated senior citizens, cower in fear, prisoners in their own homes. To all appearances, the voices of defeat have drowned out the shout of God's victory in Jesus Christ.

These are inescapable realities for anyone involved in urban ministry. Many churches, including many Lutheran churches, have struggled to strengthen the grace connection from the pulpit to the pew. There is plenty of exemplary Christian preaching by Lutherans in many cities. But the common—and false—notion persists that urban Lutheran preaching is dry, dusty, dormant, and even dead. It seemingly fails to connect; it apparently falls flat. In truth, though, urban preaching often is overwhelmed and exhausted by the climate of the city.

> *There are two things that I observe most, and I hate to stereotype. But when I listen to other Lutheran pastors, I find that many are not excited about the Gospel, so when the Gospel is preached, they try to talk about all of this as cerebral stuff. Second, for some preachers, there is no connection between mind and heart and experience. Too often, the language pastors use to communicate flows from rational, objective categories rather than their experiences.—Joseph Donnella*

An aphorism from the Middle Ages suggested that "city air makes men free." The city, with its opportunities and availability of the arts, music, and social services, gave people access to freedom. This is rarely the case in the modern context. The crises of life in modern American cities tend to imprison rather than to liberate.

The cure for spiritual defeat in the city escapes mere human solutions. Economists, politicians, and ordinary citizens have mounted soapboxes and made pronouncements on the nation's urban crisis. Words are fatigued. Leaders of every stripe agree that America's urban areas desperately need transformation. For the most part, these leaders think their own kind of talking can generate transformation. By contrast, people of the Gospel place their trust first in God's Word with its inherent dynamic potency (Romans 1:16). The Holy Spirit, working in God's words of justice and mercy, turns spiritual defeat into victory. Unless the words we use to preach derive from and are driven by God's Word, they cannot transform cities or the people languishing in their morbid maze of meaninglessness.

Pastoral Theology and Preaching

A primary purpose of doctrine is to put words—God's Word—in the preacher's mouth. All theological reflection occurs "so that we may proclaim the mystery of Christ" (Colossians 4:3). Karl Barth reminds us of the urgent placement of preaching relative to doctrine when he wrote that theology, in its broadest and truest sense, is really sermon preparation.[1] Without the careful, Confessionally grounded study of God, preaching ends up emaciated and empty. It limps along impotently. It whimpers wistfully. It cannot inspire.

Pastors are called to preach faithfully and to care compassionately for God's people. As they go about their duties, they quickly come to value the symbiosis—indeed, a mutual blessing—between faith and practice. Preaching is the vocal proclamation of God's diagnosis of and his dealings with humanity. Gospel preaching motivates hearers to embrace faithfully and passionately God's remedy in Christ. Without that Gospel Word of intervention, God's invasive action in Christ, every soul is destined for eternal death. Preaching that is pastoral and theologically grounded reaches into the places where people come face to face with the triad of sin, death, and the devil: from the luxury corner office to the lonely street corner; from the gentrified row house to the broken-down crack house; from the gated middle-class neighborhood to the vulnerable underclass public housing project. Gospel preaching touches all the places that people work, play, sleep, and pray—places where they are blessed and where they are cursed.

We need Gospel preaching because the curse of the Law is otherwise inescapable. It hammers us incessantly. It comes in dire tones of accusation and condemnation. It pounds the sting of death deep into our souls. The Confessions say it clearly. "For the law always accuses and terrifies consciences. It does not justify, because a conscience terrified by the law flees before God's judgment."[2]

The enemy of human souls, the devil, is ever the predator. Sensing faith on the ropes, he attacks like a vulture to pick apart any remaining shred of belief. Gospel preaching delivers a deathblow to the devil's power and sets the captives free.

Making All Things New

One motto for ministry that captured my imagination as I served in Detroit and that proved an effective reference for decision making was *Behold; God is doing a new thing in America's cities.* Our goal? Through the Gospel to put new hope in the heart, new discipline in life, and a new dollar in the pocket.

New Hope in the Heart

Our preaching must address and speak to the people in their day-to-day situation and give them hope— hope for a better tomorrow, assurance that God has not deserted them but that he is with them even in the struggle. And that must be key.—Ulmer Marshall Jr.

"Hope deferred makes the heart sick, but a longing fulfilled is a tree of life" (Proverbs 13:12). Langston Hughes poetically posed the same point as a question, "What happens to a dream deferred?"

> *The Word of God says something that is full of hope for our congregation. Yet five people were just shot at the bus stop across from the church. Or a family driving home is hit by another car and all four die. This is life in our cities. I struggle during the week on how to make an application of God's Word to our setting.—Donald E. Anthony*

The theology of the cross faces sin, death, and the devil squarely. Although this theology willingly embraces death, it does not end with death. The theology of the cross is a theology of hope in the resurrection. Urban conditions can be desperate and, in some cases, unjust, but suffering does not have the last word for believers. The temptation is to adopt a "victim-focused identity" from the pulpit. It is a voice marked by a hesitation to preach in such a way that the message goes the next step beyond suffering— that is, to confer Gospel power to confront and transcend human suffering. The cross, while remaining "our only theology" (Martin Luther), also stands as our only hope (*ave crux spes unica*) for transformation. In it is power and hope for overcoming destructive circumstances. The cross is a sign of God's victory in Christ, or as Eusebius called it, "the victory-giving cross."

> *Sometimes I talk about charlatans. We have a lot of them in our community too. These individuals prey on people, take their money, and leave them with very little hope. Urban people are like the old metaphor in the Scripture: lost sheep that are helpless without a shepherd. You might notice, too, that people see so much oppression, so much that belittles or depresses*

them—like billboards and advertisements. Sometimes
it's discouraging because they are unable to afford
[the things that are advertised]. Sometimes it's
harmful because the ads lead to bad health or bad
living conditions, such as tobacco, alcohol, and gam-
bling. Only the Word of God gives hope. My people
need the Word every day.—Frazier N. Odom

New Discipline in Life

Jesus taught about the prophetic nature of God's kingdom and our preparation for its consummation. "From the days of John the Baptist until now, the kingdom of heaven has been forcefully advancing, and forceful men lay hold of it" (Matthew 11:12). Believers are aggressive in hope. To continue in our calling to follow Jesus requires spiritual virtues, such as faithfulness, honor, self-control, courage, and determination. This is especially true in an urban environment with the many diversions, distortions, and literally damning devices that the devil puts in place.

Discipline and God's ordering for our freedom in Christ must be a component of urban preaching. At its verbal root, discipline is related to discipleship and learning. A Christian is a learner; Martin Luther clarifies this insight in his 95 Theses: *docendi sunt Christiani* (Christians are to be taught).[1] Being a disciple of Christ means learning, by the Spirit, to walk in the Spirit (Galatians 5:16–26). Amid the obstacles, the preacher of biblical sanctification will avoid the Charybdis of moralizing legalism, as well as the Scylla of permissive libertinism or "sloppy agape."

Most American core-city communities are in moral disarray. For this crisis, some propose esteem-based solutions, such as a form of improved psychological thinking about personal fulfillment or self-realization. From the perspective of the Gospel, this conclusion is a dead-end conundrum. Freedom is never absolute. Any attempt to be freed from God's Law re-introduces an egregious sort of tyranny. Jesus said, "If you hold to my teaching, you are really my disciples. Then you will know the truth, and the truth will set you free" (John 8:31–32). His words reveal an if/then proposition. Genuine freedom is intimately linked with truth, and truth is intimately linked with Christian discipleship and Jesus' teaching. Teaching results in discipleship, which in turn gives understanding of truth, which in turn leads to freedom. But every "turn" must be taken. No steps can be skipped. Without the Christ connection, we are left with mere philosophical truth or existential freedom. Martin H. Franzmann described this as "at best a very dubious and dangerous sort of liberty."[2] Furthermore, freedom in Christ is not something arbitrarily experienced in naked, bare power. Rather, genuine freedom encounters us—as does all truth—in Word and Sacrament. In that encounter, we are restored to God, made perfectly free, subject to no one, and placed in service to Christ and our community. We are freed to serve in the city.

A City's Story

Few things in modern life are more frightening than the seemingly irrepressible spread of urban pathology. No matter what part of the nation you are describing, the pattern is repeated. As a pastor in Detroit, I took part in developing Lutheran City Ministries, a new model for sharing and celebrating the Gospel among black, white, and Hispanic residents of that inner city. In striking ways, Detroit is a symbol of an American urban experiment gone awry. It was, therefore, an ideal "laboratory" for a creative ministry.

In the relatively short span of fifty years, Detroit has tumbled from a futuristic world-class manufacturing center to a third-world city. Like other urban areas, the city experienced remarkable growth and prosperity in the 1950s. Its population swelled to nearly two million residents. Today, Detroit is a city with less than one million residents and workers. In recent years, it has been consistently near the top of most lists of what's wrong in the nation. In the early 1990s, less than half of the city's population was in the labor force, the lowest ratio of any American city. Black men murder black men at a genocidal rate. A listing of social ills obviously would include family chaos, a deteriorating system of public education, and an unraveling community infrastructure. The quality of life has been punctured by poverty and violent crime. For many inner-city residents, hope, discipline, and dollars simply have vanished.

The spiritual ailments that lie in urban parishes (literally, *paroikia*) are much more difficult to identify. These include absurd nihilism, depersonalization, and spiritual despair. Individuals may experience a commodifying of personal worth. Self-esteem becomes connected to net worth. Possessions define the person.

> *Northside is old by Pittsburgh standards. It is racially mixed, economically mixed, and educationally mixed, on the whole a balanced neighborhood ... Almost everything positive you can think of about city life, you can find here. Almost everything negative you can think about in city life, you can find here. So it is a wonderful paradigm for urban ministry.—John R. Cochran*

Inner cities are places of rarefaction. They provide both the best of the best and the worst of the worst. Achievement seems magnified, and failure seems amplified. That's the paradox of the city.

> *I find that I often refer to addiction. Addiction is quite common in our city. It's common in our nation. Whether it's addiction to work or chemical addiction, we are addicts to all kinds of things. It's actually a very good metaphor for sin, properly understood. Also, I find myself setting up straw-man attitudes, like a propensity to violence, since these exist, especially in young people around here.—Doyle J. Theimer*

The paradoxes of Law and Gospel preaching must prevail in the paradoxical city. Both the Law and the Gospel must be connected to the culture of the city, otherwise the pulpit will not be prophetic, otherwise there is little hope in transcending specific cultures with the one truth. For example, cities characteristically have high birth rates, especially among single teenage girls. They also have high death rates, tragically among single teenage boys. An authentically urban preaching of the Law will include direct discourse on such moral matters basic to Christian ethics as: "You shall not murder." "You shall not commit adultery." Anything less than that, any polished and polite yet gutless speaking of the Law, is an act of spiritual treason. Not to hold individuals accountable for sin merely because "that's their cultural predicament" or "that's just the way those people are" is an insult to human dignity; it is a reneging of one's call to ministry. Human dignity makes no sense unless people are held accountable to God, to one another, and to themselves, no matter who they are.

One group that has struggled with disciplining and discipling its youth is the African American community. Lack of conviction and guidance from the pulpit does not help. Many preachers are unwilling, unable, or afraid to preach the Law of God fully and powerfully. Perhaps the words—spoken as imperatives—sound too harsh. Perhaps the demands appear draconian. Yet the Lutheran Confessions contend that the Law "is the thunderbolt by means of which God with one blow destroys both open sinners and false saints."[3] The prophet Jeremiah captures the force of the divine self-revelation: " 'Is not my word like fire,' declares the LORD, 'and like a hammer that breaks a rock in pieces?' " (23:29).

Shortly before his assassination, Martin Luther King Jr. wrote that self-criticism indicates maturity. He encouraged the African American community to unify and speak out about respect, sanctity of life, and the evils of gangs. He called for community agencies and programs to help black youth understand the unique attributes of urban living and improve their behavior.[4] Disciples of the Lord Jesus live in the discipline he offers and works through his Word.

A New Dollar in the Pocket

There can be no meaningful talk about urban ministry without some creative conversation about the economic reality that cripples so many inner cities. In a time of race fatigue, when old discussions have been reframed and new dialogues have been initiated across ethnic and racial lines, theological discussions also must address how we live together in time and space. Social and economic empowerment is also the task of the urban pastor; he is called to be a preacher who links the narrative of Jesus Christ to the *missio Dei* among God's people. In today's cities, this must include a prophetic element, living and working as an advocate for economic renewal as well as spiritual transformation. Under the Spirit's guidance and power, the pastor speaks the good news of the kingdom in "the face of Christ" (2 Corinthians 4:6).

> *My most immediate community, right around the church, consists of public housing for the most part. Many of the homes here are in grave disrepair. The residents are recipients of AFDC [Aid for Families with Dependent Children] and general welfare. We see panhandlers, vacant lots, empty pockets of land with no buildings, boarded up storefronts, and dilapidated buildings. Unemployment, underemployment, high school dropouts, and drive-by shootings are also all the kinds of issues that we deal with.—Frazier N. Odom*

Tonya is 37 years old. For the last eleven years she has been cleaning houses in St. Louis—sometimes two or three a day. On the hot-button topic of welfare, Tonya, in her usual blunt fashion, shared her opinion. "There are some who are poor because they want to be. But it's not really their fault. They have given up; they've lost their positive attitude. They've let the negative get in them, and that gives them low self-esteem. And they've got these daddies who don't help or won't help or can't help.

"As for me," Tonya continued, "I took one look at my two kids and I realized that $242 of aid and $120 of food stamps was not enough to make it—I had more month than I had money. So I got tired of waiting for the first of the month. I started waiting on the Lord, and God gave me the hope and power to get back to work. But I don't know what I would have done without government help, especially when my kids were little ones and I had no transportation."

Tonya's story, in many respects, is typical. We can assign blame to her irresponsible choices or to the misfortune of her circumstances, but she still ended up depending on government assistance to "make it." There are many like Tonya in our cities. Some have taken wrong turns and ended up permanent residents in shameful, painful conditions. Some are inheritors of generational dependency. Others have become ensnared in fatal attractions and now silently suffer the private drama of deferred dreams and desperation. Tonya experienced much of that.

In one respect, though, Tonya's situation is atypical. Through faith in Jesus Christ, she was able to overcome the odds. She broke through the pathology of poverty despite many who claimed she could not do it. As a child, her schools labeled her learning disabled. As an adult, her mother judged her as "unsaved" because she had given birth out of wedlock. She admittedly made mistakes. But *she* was not a mistake. Illegitimacy and poverty do not disqualify people like Tonya from forgiveness or from a place in God's kingdom.

> We see all kinds of different people. In my preaching, I relate to people who are homeless, to people who make thousands of dollars a month, and to all classes in between. So my preaching has to connect with people intellectually as well as experientially—to people who live both on and off the street.—Steven Marsh

Justice for "Just Us"?

We often preach in a manner that does not speak of the poor as having any part of "us." With ease, we exclude them from having a meaningful connection to our personal identities or our corporate identity as a family of believers. But justice is abridged if we are only thinking of "just us." Martin Luther King Jr. helped us to move out of our insulated, isolated lifestyles and into the world as a global community.

If the world were a village of ten people, we might be surprised at the living conditions of our fellow villagers:

- One would be rich

- Two would be just making it (like many of us)

- Seven would be poor

The majority on our planet does not share our identity. But Christ does identify with all of us. And His church is growing fastest in the Third World. Indeed, the center of Christianity is no longer Europe and North America. There are now more Lutherans on the continent of Africa than there are in North America. It was Asian and African bishops at the 1998 Lambeth Conference of the Episcopal Church that held the majority. As a result of this majority, Archbishop Donald Mtetemela of Tanzania amended the controversial marriage and sexuality statement offered to the conference to include the phrase that "homosexual practice is incompatible with Scripture." His conservative resolution easily passed. The Africanization of Lutheranism and Anglicanism, the Asianification of Protestantism, and the Hispanicization of Roman Catholicism are significantly changing the complexion of these churches—both literally and symbolically.

Motivated by love for the world, Christ gave his life so all people might be saved and come to a knowledge of salvation. The Holy Spirit is taking that Word to the nations of the world, and the nations are rapidly, and remarkably, responding in faith, just as in the Jerusalem church (Acts 2–6). The affluent, Western-based Christian church is being challenged to respond to the poor in our midst. Before we can work to relieve the economic hardship of other nations, we must do so at home.

In the United States, urban areas are among the hardest hit by poverty. In some areas, a majority of inner-city residents rely on some form of government assistance for their sustenance. And women and children are disproportionately represented among these poor. Detroit has the highest unemployment rate among large U.S. cities. In 1994, *Fortune* magazine suggested that Detroit was America's "Third-World City." A city with an economy comparable to a developing nation should call attention to a moral dilemma for the only remaining superpower nation of the first world, especially because of the proximity of Ford, General Motors, and Chrysler, which are returning record profits.

But economic hardship does not strike only in urban areas. The Rev. Norman Sincebaugh, president of The Lutheran Church—Missouri Synod's North Dakota District, describes the 650,000 residents of that state as mostly farmers. Many are hardened veterans in a declining agrarian industry. In 1996, 125,000 cattle perished because of devastating floods, blizzards, and hailstorms—losses that have decimated the state's agricultural base. Coupled with a dwindling tax base, the pressure on churches to respond in rural America also has risen.

Theological Dimensions of Poverty

The Old Testament contains more legal and prophetic material about the poor and the powerless than about other societal problem. In both narrative and prophetic texts, a strong relationship exists between righteousness—the cornerstone of the Christian doctrine of justification—and justice. In Hebrew and Greek, *righteousness* and *justice* share root words. As justified believers—made right with God entirely through Jesus Christ—our attitude toward and treatment of the poor is a fundamental justice question. Questions of justice inevitably flow from the faith of the justified ones. God says to His people, "Therefore, I command you to be openhanded toward your brother and toward the poor and needy in the land" (Deuteronomy 15:11). When the weak are oppressed and the needs of the poor come to God's attention, the psalmist writes that God "will now arise ... I will protect them from those who malign them" (Psalm 12:5).

More than half of Jesus' parables (17 of the 29 in the synoptic gospels) concern money. These parables lay out the perils of misplaced priorities; they are stories of the disordered, upside-down lives of people whose long-term "investments" expire prematurely. Jesus urges his disciples to invest in the kingdom, in God's people, in those who are poor and needy in the eyes of the world. Followers of Jesus stock up on true righteousness and justice, rather than on riches that rust or fade away.

God's Word addresses situations that sound similar to our modern context:

- If there is a poor man among your brothers in any of the towns of the land that the LORD your God is giving you, do not be hardhearted or tightfisted toward your poor brother. (Deuteronomy 15:7)

- Do not take advantage of a hired man who is poor and needy, whether he is a brother Israelite or an alien living in one of your towns. (Deuteronomy 24:14)

- Do not deprive the alien or the fatherless of justice, or take the cloak of the widow as a pledge. (Deuteronomy 24:17)

In Psalm 41:1 we hear a beatitude of brotherly love: "Blessed is he who has regard for the weak." In any society, there will be those who are too weak to "make it"—those who aren't strong or resilient enough, who aren't skilled or tough-willed, who lack the "right stuff" or the right connections. Such individuals often are marginalized. We see, all too clearly, where they stand. The question is, Where do we stand? Do we stand with them?

These are strange times to be doing urban ministry. Across the length and the breadth of the land, there is

*a weariness with the issues that deeply affect cities.
And that calls for special devotion on the part of the
church. We don't blow with the wind. We are not on
today and off tomorrow. The commitment of the
church to the poor is inherent in the Gospel, no matter what is happening in the current social and political winds or in the economic sphere. We don't lose
heart because the One who charts the course is the
Lord, not the politicians or pollsters. Our calling is to
be in the city for the people, with the people, no matter what is going on politically or socially.—John R.
Cochran*

As God's redeemed people, we have the calling—and opportunity—to be openhanded and tenderhearted toward those in
need, not hard-hearted and tightfisted. LCMS Eastern District
President David Belasic suggests that God is favorably biased
toward the poor, toward those who are suffering, toward those
who have been shattered by the vicissitude of life. God cares. His
people care too.

The Relativizing of Compassion

The crisis of postmodern truth decay is dangerous for the
poor. Not only have the philosophical virtues of prudence, honor,
self-control, and courage been undermined by cultural relativism,
but the impetus to care for others, which derives ultimately from a
biblical ethic of love for neighbor, is rapidly eroding. Laws that pro-
hibit the taking of life are part of the biblical tradition.

Without the cultivation of these values and virtues, moral
solipsism will prevail. With the unraveling of a moral base, "might
makes right" (following Faust's Mephistopheles) becomes the basis
for making decisions. The "will to power" (Nietzsche) becomes the
basis for action. Compassion is incompatible with such a relativiz-
ing of morality. For relationships of care to arise and grow, there

must be a moral standard.

Besides the relationship between justification and justice, there is a point at which poverty and the sanctity of life intersect. Since human life is a gift of God, it is inherently holy. The notion of idly standing by and letting some people live like hell, in a human hell, only to die and go to hell is a faith question. C. S. Lewis once said that next to the Lord's Supper, the most sacred thing is the person next to you.[5] For people who place their faith and life in Christ, poverty is not a socioeconomic issue nor a political problem. Poverty is a moral question, a theological issue. Our lives are not merely biological or social or political. How we share life is primarily about theology; it is a God issue. Life, from conception to natural death, is a gift from God. And God cares about the poor.

Sanctity of life is a risky topic, but urban churches will not long be able to maintain their silence on the pro-life question. Too many voices from the city have shown convincingly how the abortion business seems to target directly inner cities, in particular Hispanic and African American communities. There seems to be an ample availability of Planned Parenthood clinics in the ghetto. For example, there are approximately 33 million blacks in the United States today. Without abortion, which has been legal since 1973, there would be nearly 50 million African Americans. Some protesters have called this biomedical genocide.

How we live together, then, and how we preserve the inherent holiness of human life is fundamental to our confession of faith. It is also a bottom-line principle of diversity. Treating some people as ostensibly dispensable is contrary to the will of God: "The Lord is not slow in keeping his promise, as some understand slowness. He is patient with you, not wanting anyone to perish, but everyone to come to repentance" (2 Peter 3:9). As Stanley Hauerwas states: "Our task, as Christians, is not to offer … theoretical alternatives, but rather to be an alternative. Christians provided such an alternative when they thought it a good thing to construct houses of hospitality for people who would have otherwise died alone. Christians provided such alternatives when they did not kill their children who were born deformed."[6]

Not preaching on the tough topic of poverty can be a sin of omission. Martin Luther says, "God rightly calls all persons murderers who do not offer counsel and aid to men in need."[7] Our Lord himself strongly identifies with human need in the parable of the sheep and goats: "I was hungry and thirsty, I was a stranger and naked, I was sick and in prison and you did not feed me, welcome me, clothe me, or visit me." (See Matthew 25:31–46.) France has enshrined this concept of meeting human need in its legal code, making it a criminal offense not to aid a person in mortal danger. Jesus implicated the Levite and the priest of this very offense as they passed by the injured man in the story of the Good Samaritan.

The Morality of Charity

Alexis de Tocqueville, on his nine-month tour of America in the 1800s, was astounded by the generosity of Americans. As he recounted the kindness and care he witnessed, he noted how it flowed from a living faith among these early Americans. Charity formed authentic relational bonds, nurtured and sustained by care and compassion. In this personal, face-to-face charity, de Tocqueville found a basis for a mutually redemptive sharing between the giver and the receiver. In contrast to state or agency "intervention," when individuals attempt to ameliorate the condition of a poor person, they intimately involve themselves in the outcome of that person's life. When the needy person is overwhelmed with gratitude, he or she responds to the giver. Thus a personal moral tie is established.

In Psalm 9:18, concern for the sick is blended with compassion for the poor: "The needy will not always be forgotten, nor the hope of the afflicted ever perish." Whether poverty of spirit leads to material poverty or vice-versa does not matter. What matters are churches that appear handcuffed in dealing with poverty.

In February 1998, H. George Anderson, presiding bishop of the Evangelical Lutheran Church in America, suggested that as Christianity is increasingly pressed away from the center to the margins of Western civilization, Christians will become increasingly empathetic in sharing the suffering of those whose existence is eked out on the fringes. Rather than the institution providing charity in a top-down manner, it will occur at the grass roots—people helping people, face to face, in solidarity.[8]

> *Sadly, we have a great deal of apathy towards what is going on in the community and the city at large.—Donald E. Anthony*

When anointed with "very expensive perfume" before his passion, Jesus spoke what has become an aphorism for modern people: "The poor you will always have with you" (Matthew 26:11). Contrary to popular belief, his words are not a rationale for resignation to cold, hard reality: "Since there will always be poverty, it doesn't make any sense to try to do or say anything about it." Jesus is not proposing a plank for passivity toward the poor or making a case for silence no more than he suggests that we cease resisting temptation since it remains ever before us. Our Lord's words affirm our priorities of faith living: first, toward God in lives of praise, then toward our neighbor in lives of love. The pervasive problem of poverty does not provide an escape or an excuse, but to the person of faith, it is an invitation to action. The problem of the poor is a preachable topic. For urban pulpits to maintain integrity, economic questions must be viewed through a spiritual lens.

> *Seventy percent of people living in this section of Mobile need some type of public assistance. Crime of all kinds, gangs, drugs, open selling of dope on the street corners—we have all that. Robbery, theft, teenage pregnancy, drop outs from school—it's all here.—Ulmer Marshall Jr.*

Violence, injustice, the crisis of dependency, and legitimate paths toward empowerment are themes to be addressed squarely in prophetic urban pulpits. Preachers motivate and inspire God's people to service in these arenas. In their seminal historical study, C. Eric Lincoln and Lawrence Mamiya recount the legacy of social preaching in the African American church. They note that black preachers covered a variety of topics in their public addresses, including economic issues, educational issues, employment issues, and family issues.[9]

Globally, the population of cities increases one quarter million people per day. In 1900, only one in ten people lived in cities. Now 50 percent of the earth's population live inside city limits or in close proximity to cities. In a short span of time, that percentage will increase to include the vast majority of those who dwell on earth. While global urbanization is accelerating, many aspects of urban life are not keeping pace.

Millennia of agricultural-based villages and 250 years of industrial-based economies have come to a screeching halt in our technology-based world. In few places has the change been more apparent than in the city. In an electronic age, information is the dominant currency. Once more, cities prove poorest; they have little capital to work with or to offer. American cities stand in need of technology-based investment.

Our current consideration of life in inner cities cannot overlook the social and political attempts to initiate renewal. The quest by federal, state, and local governments to renew urban communities has been frustrating and disappointing for residents, social engineers, and many well-intentioned politicians. In 1949, the federal government launched a program called Urban Renewal. It took fifteen years for anyone to notice that this program destroyed neighborhoods and decimated what had been an intact sense of community. Urban Renewal revitalized nothing. A follow-up initiative, the Community Action Program (begun in 1964), was quickly disbanded and succeeded by Model Cities in 1966. Since then, visions and strategies have come and gone:

- Community Development Block Grants (1974)
- Urban Development Action Grants (1977)
- Enterprise Zones (1980)

- Empowerment Zones (1995)

- The Personal Work and Responsibility Act (more widely known as Welfare Reform) (1996)

The *New York Times Magazine* recently issued a stinging indictment: "It is therefore extremely difficult to find statistical evidence that any inner-city neighborhood in the country has been revitalized."[10]

Some estimate the dollars already spent by government-peddled programs to help cities at 5.5 trillion. Black economist Thomas Sowell disagrees with the assumption that "top-down" programs or policies can transform cities: "The assumption that spending more of the taxpayers' money will make things better has survived all kinds of evidence that it has made things worse. The black family—which survived slavery, discrimination, poverty, wars, and depressions—began to come apart as the federal government moved in with its well-financed programs to 'help.' "[11]

> *There's a mind-set or an attitude in New York City that leaves people very close to the edge. We have a lot of lower-income neighborhoods, and we have a lot of discouragement. People are demoralized, especially if they can't find work or if they don't want to work. Many people are like one paycheck away from being out on the street. They're scrambling like crazy to make ends meet, to make a life for themselves. New York is very close to the American dream because it's all around you—it's just across the river. You see it every day. It also has a very worldly spirit especially as compared to the Midwest. It's easy to get sidetracked and lose the integrity of your mission.—Doyle J. Theimer*

The Preferred "Preferred Future"

While poverty will persist until Jesus comes again, the church of Jesus Christ is called to work aggressively to alleviate the suffering of the poor. The hunger of the poor is also spiritual; it is for the Good News (Luke 4:18–19). God's people have ample opportunity to be the fulfillment of Scripture among the poor. This is the preferred future for this world.

In the final analysis, however, the picture of the future we most prefer is the one seen by John in his vision in the book of Revelation. He sees another economic system where the curse of death is reversed for everyone, where healing and recovery are the new order. This image encompasses the problem of urban poverty. In John's vision, there is a garden. In the garden, there is a tree with leaves for the healing of the nations—literally, for the therapy of the ethnics, which is for every nation, every tribe, every people, and every language. These healed ethnics are standing before the throne and singing their songs and shouting their victory: "Amen! Praise and glory and wisdom and thanks and honor and power and strength be to our God for ever and ever. Amen!" (7:12). Until that day, we work and pray and preach. For there is no working, praying, or preaching in heaven, only rejoicing and rest.

Dangerous
Disconnections

If you understand Lutheran theology, you want to understand the streets and the people who live here. Connect, connect, connect!—John R. Cochran

In God's world, nothing exists or happens in a vacuum. Martin Luther describes the creaturely matter of this world as Creator-made: The stuff of life is to "help provide the comforts and necessities of life."[1] The creature comforts we make and use are not themselves evils to be avoided, but they are resources that help us praise and glorify God. To paraphrase Saint Augustine's maxim: Using the world is what the good do in order that they may enjoy God; using God is what the evil do in order that they may enjoy the world. Lutherans embrace the call of the First Article of the

Apostles' Creed to "enjoy" God by using his gifts in this world.

Who has not been awestruck when viewing aesthetically magnificent architecture in a house of worship—the lovely dwelling-place built to the glory of God? Whose skin has not tingled when strolling through a beautiful basilica? Whose eyes have not welled up with tears, overflowing with heartfelt joy, as a musical masterpiece is sung in praise to the Lord? We do not spurn the good things God gives us to use. Matter matters to God. What a blessed opportunity to make matter matter more in the cities. Urban preachers are called to speak the creative Word so the Good News invites hearers to a higher level of valuing their community, their environment, and their possessions.

This embrace of the First Article is one of the Christian church's gifts for the cities of America. Tragically, some facilely pass over God the Creator. In the more radical charismatic or Pentecostal Christianity, the tendency is to pit the Second and Third articles against the First Article. The mediating dimensions of the Gospel, preaching, Baptism, and the Lord's Supper are de-emphasized; the preference for God is known primarily—some say exclusively—in his unmediated, direct, naked revelation. Nothing earthly, human or created, gets in the way of knowing God and being known by him. Thus, a hyperspiritualization disregards the context of creation—the neighborhoods, homes, yards, and buildings where people live and work. Tragically, these are avoided and replaced with a "heightened" sense of God. It is a dualism that blunts ministry to the whole person and the whole community.

In some urban churches (even those located in bare bones, dilapidated storefront buildings) the preaching consists, in large part, of a verbal assault on the inherent evil of the physical world. Since the things of this world are so implacably beyond repair, salvation is spoken of as commensurate with detachment from the world. "If you're truly saved," the message seems to shout, "you won't care about, attend to, approve of, or as much as smile at anything of this world."

God's heart is broken; God weeps; God mourns. At

the demise of the first human [siblings]—the Cain and Abel story—God asks Cain, "Where is your brother? Your brother's blood is crying out to me from the ground." We somehow lose the pain and the joy when our preaching is purely abstract.—Joseph Donnella

In a way far beyond what we can recognize or sense, God cares about the things of this world. He sees all that is rotten with sin and still makes his face to shine on us. God is distressed when his creation is afflicted (Isaiah 63:9). Sin breaks the heart of God, especially when it is directed at the innocent, when children or the powerless are involved. "If anyone causes one of these little ones who believe in me to sin, it would be better for him to be thrown into the sea with a large millstone tied around his neck" (Mark 9:42). Sin is serious to God. The pastor's struggle is to prepare and preach a message that reflects God's heart.

Disconnection, connectedness. What was really powerful Sunday was that we had everybody into it. The "dry bones" was a real powerful image. Of course we sang the spiritual "Dry Bones." God connects them dry bones. That's part of that whole notion in the body of Christ. He connects all of us in Baptism.— Carlos Hernandez

Exegizing the Context

One of the things we have intentionally decided is to use the lectionary. We are not moving away from the lectionary as some churches are; we believe that God is going to speak through those readings. What that involves in terms of preparation is staying very

*close to members, receiving their phone calls, hearing
their issues, talking to them about their life issues,
and then being very intentional in seeing how the
texts in the lectionary impinge on those life issues. It
is a process where we do the Bible work and the lectionary work and then we go and see what is happening in the lives of people. It sets a context for proclamation.—Victor J. Belton*

Seminary faculties do well the important work of forming
pastors with exegetical skills. The study, interpretation, and communication of the Bible is an essential skill for the called servant of
God. This includes knowing how ancient geographical, historical,
and social factors impact the biblical text. Only after such research
is the preacher ready to preach. As Gerhard Forde succinctly puts
it: "Preaching is basically a 'doing' of the text to the hearers."[2]

Preaching is also a "doing" of the community from God's
perspective. It is speaking that makes public God's righteous read-
ing of the community. Preachers, then, connect to the community
as part of the world that God has made. They delve deeply into the
geographical, historical, and social context of those to whom the
message is intended and delivered.

*In the process of sermon preparation, a preacher is
best equipped if he knows what's going on. I mean,
whether we are talking about some murders or some
shootings or some similar incidents.—James Capers*

Big, Burning Culture Questions

Questions surrounding culture and multiculturalism have
become burning, burdensome, and hotly contested issues in society and the church. Culture, according to Samuel Huntington, will
be the key battleground for future warfare. A driving cultural com-

ponent will be religion because it encourages and inspires people.[3] The church is invariably enmeshed in this clash.

The Bible has no specific word for culture, though there is plenty of cultural content. Scripture does speak of the elements of culture: world (*cosmos* or *oikoumene*), nation (*ethnos*), custom (*ethos*), generation (*genea*), tribe (*phyle*), people (*laos*), religion or the externals of worship (*threskeia*), form (*morphe*), and language (*glossa*). Within a conservative Lutheran framework, the discussion of culture is further impeded because the Confessional writings offer no direct doctrine of culture. In truth, no single article of faith—God, Christ, salvation—can interpret the multicultural pluralism of our day. There are, however, numerous entries into culture through the doctrine of the Church, Law and Gospel, the Two Kingdoms, and the Sacraments.

Baptism into Christ and into the community of those who gather in his name is entrance into a distinct subculture. This does not solve the dilemma of distinguishing Christ and culture. To effectively distinguish Christ and culture, preachers must have an ear for the myriad sounds of the culture in all its muddling forms. Indeed, there is much confusing talk coming from many quarters in the culture debates. Gospel preachers will identify what is of God and what is not. Another sound they must interpret is the clash of the meeting between historic Christianity—with its European heritage—and the emerging Christian movement among those whose cultural base is not European. Scripture and the Confessions are the navigation system to aid interpreters in making these distinctions.

Paul Raabe suggests that the Christ/culture dialogue is best viewed as a dynamic tension to be held in a balanced perspective:

- At times, Christianity *affirms* culture: "Whatever is true, whatever is noble, whatever is right, whatever is pure, whatever is lovely, whatever is admirable—if anything is excellent or praiseworthy—think about such things" (Philippians 4:8).

- At times, Christianity *opposes* culture: There are times a prophetic word against oppression, injustice, or sinful popular opinion must be spoken. "The antithesis between God and culture runs throughout the story of Israel, Jesus, and the early church."

- At times, Christianity *leavens* culture: There are times to be salt and light, times to be transformative presences in a sin-formed world.

- At times, Christianity *employs* culture: There are times to identify with a people, to be in solidarity with their human struggle, to borrow from their resources and cultural reserves, and to use their gifts in service of the Gospel.[4]

Thomas Sowell calls this sort of understanding and reciprocity "cultural capital."[5] In other words, we all are enriched by the diverse cultural investment brought by immigrants. Whether they come from Accra or Saxony, their gifts of food, music, opinion, and ethos have not fragmented us but have made us a freer, better people. Furthermore, it is the function of the state to protect the conditions that allow an autonomous functioning of smaller, beneficial socioethnic units—what Richard John Neuhaus and others have called "mediating structures."

In the church, we are enriched, catholicity is expanded, spirituality is deepened, and the Gospel is furthered when we share the cultural gifts found in the diversity of people in Christ's church. These are our common gifts. The more time we spend together appreciating our diversity and praising God for it, the less we are likely to diminish anyone. We soon learn that the notion that one group has an inherently superior culture amounts to nothing more than windbag oratory.

There is an inevitability to culture. One cannot help but speak from one's cultural experience. Nathan Mitchell defines culture as "all those forces—personal and collective, public and private—that shape social identity, transmit shared values, and determine how we define *other* people, places, things, and events."[6] Wherever we find human life, we find culture.

The Augsburg Confession maintains that "it is sufficient [*satis est*] for the true unity of the Christian church that the Gospel be preached in conformity with a pure understanding of it and that the sacraments be administered in accordance with the divine Word"[7] These are the Church's proper tools. In contrast, "It is not necessary [*non necesse est*] for the true unity of the Christian church that ceremonies, instituted by men, should be observed uniformly in all places."[8]

"Word and Sacrament ministry" is a phrase that has become more and more alive for me. I find this focus works well in an African American neighborhood: Christ coming to us, not only in the spoken and also "invisible" Word but in the simple, visible words of Baptism and the Lord's Supper. As we celebrate the Sacraments, we are reminded of who we are.—Steven Marsh

What we mean by vernacular, then, encompasses much more than being idiomatic, down to earth, cool, or cute with language. *Vernacular* means that the sights and sounds and senses of Scripture are communicated intelligibly in clear words, in ordinary bread and wine, in simple water. Cultural communication pays attention to the song, drama, music, dance, poetry, art, emotion, and colors that are important to a people.

Images of the day of Pentecost come to mind because New York has about 175 different spoken languages. You walk around in the community and hear languages that you cannot understand.—Steven Marsh

Participants know the vernacular when they see it, taste it, or feel it. C. S. Lewis once wrote: "You must translate every bit of your Theology into the vernacular. This is very troublesome and it means you can say very little in half an hour."[9] (Now it's 12 minutes or less!) Lewis contends that the vernacular is essential. "I have come to the conviction that if you cannot translate your thoughts into uneducated language, then your thoughts were confused. Power to translate is the test of having really understood one's own meaning."[10] In other words, divine truth in ordinary words.

> Sometimes we get so carried away with using big words that we bury the true Word of God. We can't add anything to God's Word. We don't need to take anything [away]; we just need to say it like it is. Plain and simple. —Ulmer Marshall Jr.

Is *Diversity* a Dirty Word?

When I arrived on campus for college orientation, I was barraged with the usual ream of official forms, including one that provided demographic data for the student body. I've always considered my cultural diversity a blessing. Because of my pride, or perhaps the cynicism of late adolescence, I searched for the categories that defined me. I found several. Under race, I checked both the white and black boxes to represent both of my parents. As a carrier of a Portuguese ancestral name, I checked the Spanish-surnamed box. As a Jamaican-born, Canadian citizen (at that time), I also checked the international student box. "This won't do," advised the college official. "We'd appreciate it if you would narrow this down." I landed on the black category because that is the cultural group to which I most closely relate. This was also easiest because the majority of blacks in the United States have racially mixed backgrounds. Most so-called "African Americans" also have white or American Indian blood. Likewise, many who appear "white" would be surprised by their genetic mix.

Since that formative event, I've done a lot of thinking, praying, teaching, and preaching about race, culture, and identity. Is there a Christian prism through which we can view these issues?

Our age is highly charged. Many are fed up and frustrated by the seeming impossibility of racial reconciliation. The divisions and distinctions between people groups seem more amplified than ever.

Pittsburgh's not quite as fast-paced and crazy as the coastal cities—not as broadly diverse as the larger cities. It's pretty much a question of black and white. It's also pretty much the old question of how do we deal with one another—live together and worship together—in this kind of a neighborhood.—John R. Cochran

Caution must be used as we delicately make our way over this burning culture question. There are twin pitfalls as we broach the discussion. Cultural isolationism, on the one hand, and cultural syncretism, on the other, make the preacher easy prey for heresy. Isolationism detaches God's people from history and its multifaceted tapestry. Syncretism saturates the truth with human—often false—elements that eventually water down the message. A biblical understanding of the vernacular carefully balances the two. It follows Paul's maxim in 1 Thessalonians 5:21: "Test everything. Hold on to the good." On the one hand, responsible exegesis and preaching does not simply genuflect at the altar of tradition, especially when customs or ceremonies impede the free course of the Gospel. The Lutheran Reformers opposed those who negated the Word of God by imposing traditions. On the other side, the exegete's hand moves defensively when dealing with those who despise and devalue the role of religious tradition, who do not revere "the faith that was once for all entrusted to the saints" (Jude 3).

I happen to believe that Martin Luther was one of the premier "contextualizationists." He took the Word and he made sure that those who were hearing it heard it in their own language, in their own cul-

tural background. He did it so that they could hear it on their own level. I happen to believe that Martin Luther would laugh at a group of African American Lutherans sitting around singing only German hymns when our whole tradition is so rich. As African American Lutherans, we can take our place in the African American church by trying to contextualize Word and Sacrament ministry. It is very powerful.—Steven Marsh

Evangelical contextualization is a deep, discerning, and thoughtful exercise, one that is never rushed into and never finished. Many Christians feel a sense of fatigue with the sociopolitical opinions concealed in religious language and symbols. People are hungering and thirsting for spiritual substance, not simply trite generalizations. Stanley Hauerwas notes: "That is why the sermon meant to illumine our condition, which is often eloquent and profound, is also so forgettable and even boring. Insights about the human condition are a dime a dozen. Most days most of us would rightly trade any insight for a good meal."[11]

Pulpits have power as they connect the heart of God's truth with the hearts of broken humanity through the heart of pastoral integrity. Is *diversity* a dirty word? No, but it is not a clean word. If it requires the sacrifice of your integrity as a pastor. A significant part of your calling involves knowing those to whom you are speaking. To know their spiritual condition and sacramental needs. To recognize that without Christ, they are all the same: lost and condemned sinners. Preaching with pastoral integrity means speaking the Word amid difficult and diverse contexts.

In this neighborhood, for example, probably 60 to 75 percent of all people are unbaptized. You may not assume that you are dealing with a mature community of faith. You may not assume that you are dealing with committed Christians. You are, instead,

speaking to a mixed group of hearers every time.—
John R. Cochran

Clashing of Kingdoms

All people groups possess a God-given cultural capital. Each has unique life experiences that enrich all. This is the contribution these groups make to the church catholic. Yet the Word says all have sinned, all have fallen far short of God's glory (Romans 3:23). Especially in these times when some are fixated on an almost utopian innocence of cultural groups, a word of Law will expose this myth. Some have chosen not to confront unduly proud attitudes of racial supremacy. By not doing so, they acquiesce to a naive type of racial essentialism that invariably denies original sin. When certain ethnic groups claim God made them inherently superior, they falsify God's Word. God does not play favorites.

Preachers long have translated the ancient Word into fresh word pictures that enfranchise the hearer and provoke—deliberately—an affirmation of faith, an "Amen." From this rhythm arises a participatory proclamation, an antiphonal "call and response" sent forth by the preacher and talked back by the congregation. This dialogue involves more than a mere outward stylistic technique. It is a process of translating the Word conversationally, that is, preaching with hearing foremost in mind.

A Race Myth

Some of the biblical images that I find relevant are the stories in the early chapters of Genesis that talk about the cultivation of civilization. It's an obvious fact that all human beings are related as human beings. We share a common parentage; no matter where we are on the globe, we all have the same parents essentially. That realization is important in an urban context.—Joseph Donnella

Tragically, racism is an historically justified and socially structured attitude that leads to hostility, discrimination, and, at times, full-fledged persecution. Some would even argue that systems, including denominations, can be inherently—though not purposively—racist. For example, most Lutheran congregations and church bodies in the United States were created by and for European immigrants; thus, the perception is that Lutheran churches can be nothing but racist. This view fails because, at the root, denominations are not brought into being for the preservation of an attitude, but for a spiritual identity and for the sake of propagating the Gospel.

Racism is sin because it violates the Redeemer's intent: God the Savior wants all people to be saved (1 Timothy 2:4). Racism is an attack on both the soteriological "first principle" and the human condition. It only can be countered with a spiritually constructed story that begins with incarnation and culminates in baptismal incorporation into the saving Lord. No human design or accomplishment can erase the spirit of racism from our midst. It is too deeply ingrained; it is too natural to our fallen humanity. Humans are powerlessly sinful. It is too easy to discriminate, to prefer some and oppress others on the basis of such an obvious externality as skin color. Yet the Gospel holds the promise of power to transform and rebuild.

> *I suppose that Lutheran theology would acknowl-*
> *edge racism as a sin that is prevalent. It's a reality*
> *that we have to experience, and yet while it's a reali-*
> *ty, it's not something that we have to succumb to. Its*
> *power has been broken. The power of Christ has*
> *enabled us to find ways to deal with it, to overcome*
> *it, not to be hindered by it. We don't have to remain*
> *hindered by it. Again I believe the Gospel that we*
> *proclaim [as] the Lutheran Church is available to*
> *all people, regardless of what racism might say or*
> *teach. Racism is a lie. It's just not true. And that's*
> *what we teach in the church, and we don't need to*
> *put up with it, and we don't have to succumb to it.—*
> *Donald E. Anthony*

Only as we develop testimonies of our baptismal incorporation into the body of Christ—the quintessential family—will we deconstruct the myth of race.

Racial essentialism is closely related to ethnocentrism. People inclined toward an ethnocentric bias equate their point of view with absolute truth. Radical forms of racial centrism view the world through the group's eyes only. Militant monoculturalists on the right want to impose their cultural forms, music, and leadership style on the church. They fail to distinguish theology and culture. In American Christianity, this sometimes has taken the form of implicitly extolling the allegedly superior virtues of European civilization. Often this subconsciously is done without an awareness of the hidden presuppositions. On the other hand, militant multiculturalists on the left want to ignore the past (and great) contributions of dead, white European males whom they consider deplorable. Adherents to this belief falsely build the self-esteem of minorities by telling them how pristine and utopian their traditional religion was prior to its "infection" by Christianity. Both the monocultural and the multicultural ideologue distort and corrupt the message of Christ and Christian tradition. Both issue forth from a crisis of vision.

Evidence suggests that being black in America is much more about culture than it is about race. Race has very little inborn, inherent, or ontological significance. Racial essentialism is indefensible as an argument for the moral superiority or inferiority of any race. We all have met devils and angels of every color, class, and culture. Essentialism runs the risk of reducing everything that we are to a string of stereotypes and tired anecdotes.

Ethan Bronner, writing in the *New York Times*, suggests that historians and scientists are increasingly of the opinion that the concept of "race" is a thoroughly modern development and one that lacks biological support.[1] Apart from obvious physical differences, one might even wonder whether races actually exist. With so many individuals who shatter our notions of race (such as Tiger Woods) and with such a high level of sharing of cultural forms, we might be confronted with more exceptions to any definition of race than rules. Pigeonholing people and categorizing by race clearly presents problems.

Some private and public groups—perhaps even states and nations—may have a stake in overrating questions of race. (I will refrain from mentioning the horrific examples of discrimination, persecution, and genocide in our century.) This is why we need the church's voice. The true church always stands against racial discrimination. We are a community that embraces the teachings of Jesus, whose Word transforms human hearts and inaugurates a vision for reconciliation and renewal. At the foot of the cross, in the waters of Baptism, at the table of the Lord, in the family of the forgiven, hostilities cease. Here, among the holy people of God, all life is sacred.

The Missionary to All Humanity

The incarnation of Jesus is a prototypical cross-cultural missionary action. Jesus remains the missionary to all humanity. In this primary sending, the Father purposefully sent the Son of God and of Man "to seek and to save what was lost" (Luke 19:10). Jesus' mission statement focused on the Father's "preferred destiny" for all humanity. To save us, Jesus became a part of a specific human community located at a multicultural crossroad. This was not incidental, but central to Jesus' person and work. God purposefully chose the multicultural, multiracial, multilingual eastern Mediterranean to be the context for the sending of his Son. From the crossroad of that diverse world, his Word radiated into all the world. America is strikingly similar in its richly textured diversity.

> *I love the understanding that we are saint and sinner at the same time. That helps me get over my initial reluctance to embrace my brother. I recognize that my failures are part of my sinful nature. I don't need to try and justify this activity or that attitude.*
>
> *At the same time, I don't necessarily have to allow it to paralyze me because I'm also a saint, forgiven and empowered by Christ. That is a motivating force for me—to be the person that God has called me to be in Jesus.—James A. Wetzstein*

As a rabbi standing to read the sacred Scriptures, Jesus' words in Hebrew were likely "translated" into the vernacular, into the language of the home, which was Aramaic. When he offered himself as an unblemished human sacrifice for sin, the place of his execution bore a mini-billboard that announced Pilate's mocking, yet accurate, verdict in three languages. No culture is excluded from the creative or the redemptive activity of God.

At the crossroad of this culture war, some are courageously seeking to cut an alternative path—a better way of love for the sake of reaching all people. "The very nature of the Gospel imperative necessitates the heralding of the once-for-all reconciling act of God in Christ Jesus in words and forms that have the potential to reach the hearts and ears of the listener."[2] Of course, the content of the faith—what we preach—must remain squarely rooted within the framework of the ancient canon: "We should hold fast to what has been believed everywhere, always and by everyone" (*quod semper, quod ubique, quod ab omnibus creditum est*). But to say that culture is always an impediment or an obstacle to the Gospel is to deny that human means for its proclamation. The Church lives and works in multicultural, multiracial, and multilingual settings.

Many younger blacks and Hispanics (and some frustrated and angry whites) are retreating from the mainstream of American life into race-based enclaves. Formally, this movement is sometimes called "critical race theory." Its adherents (young college-age non-Anglos) are finding in this theory an intellectual foundation for newly flourishing forms of separateness. In academic settings, this might involve separate dorms, fraternities, academic programs, and even commencement activities.

Critical race theory derives from some of the same sources of thought as postmodern scholarship. Drawing on anti-Western ideology, critical race theory suggests that there is no rationale or legitimacy to the Church's mission across race lines because it is impossible for any one group to identify with the experience of another group. The walls rise strong and high. Ideally, each race stands alone.

Dinesh D'Souza probably overstates the case, but his critique is compelling. In summary, he says: "[B]lack culture also has a vicious, self-defeating, and repellent underside that it is no longer possible to ignore or euphemise. As more and more blacks seem to realize, no good is achieved by dressing these pathologies in sociological cant, complete with the familiar vocabulary of disadvantage and holding society to account."[3]

We preach the sense of restoration in the middle of decay and the impact that promise of the future has

*on the present life. I'm always clear to help folks
understand that we are not going to embark on a
program to create heaven on earth. If we think that
we are walking out the door to bring the kingdom of
God and all its perfection into our community, we
are going to be sadly disappointed. But the kingdom
is about knowing who we are, that we are members of
God's kingdom.—James A. Wetzstein*

Christian theologians must reflect creatively on political and social justice and renewal, but the nature and goal of this reflection and proclamation must remain Gospel-centered. By God's grace, the aim is to reach people and convert them from sin and death to the way of salvation, which is theirs only through faith in Jesus Christ. By grace, those who have been catechized and confirmed in the faith are nurtured in their life in Christ for service to their communities.

The means used are primary tools: preaching, baptizing, receiving the Lord's Supper, hearing the Word of forgiveness, and sharing in the mutual strengthening among believing sisters and brothers. The Gospel is spoken in these many ways because "God is surpassingly rich in his grace."[4] In this way, the kingdom of God comes into our midst. Its advent is seldom smooth, seldom easy, by our standards. The kingdom of God scrapes and tears when divine truth enters into people of sin. But the kingdom soothes and heals, too, when the Gospel makes "everything new" (Revelation 21:5).

Tumbling Walls

A new form of urban housing is the gated community. Here walls (and fences) protect the law-abiding from the terror of urban villainy. Such hyperseparation (and segregation) is a dangerous sign for the health of race relations.

To be sure, a divided environment may have a socially nurturing function. Targeting a historically alienated group is often a compensatory goal for institutional leaders. African American colleges provide a positive example. These institutions have generated a competent base of leadership through nurturing homogenous, "radically safe" environments. This is borne out in the attrition and graduation rates of African American college students. Approximately 15 percent of African American students are enrolled in historically black colleges and universities. This 15 percent accounts for more than 50 percent of African American college graduates.

Howard University has a student body of approximately 12,000 students. Approximately one half of the students are international students from the African continent. The rest are African Americans, primarily, and they are from the U.S., although some are from the Caribbean and South America as well. The climate here is diverse, strong, and good.—Joseph Donnella

A diversity of people is perhaps the characteristic most apparent in the urban setting. Poverty appears in many parts of America—in cities, in suburbs, and in rural communities such as Appalachia or the Mississippi Delta. Crime is becoming more commonplace, even in low-risk "monolithic" suburban communities. But a range of people groups and a variety of lifestyles and ethnic backgrounds best describe and typify modern cities.

We see a wide range of people in urban churches. There are educational backgrounds that go as far as graduate degrees, as well as some people who are not well educated and live right in the community.— Donald E. Anthony

The reconciliation won by Christ on the cross restores the vertical relationship between God and humanity. This reconciliation also extends horizontally to brothers and sisters of every race, binding God's people in Christian love. As this love breaks down the walls that divide and forms ties that bind, we move closer to a post-hyphenated community.

Discussion of an authentic Christian community is a risky topic these days. Such conversation does not fit into postmodern times. We like to think we are beyond such a primitive concept as "Christian community," that we are too psychologically adjusted, too technologically sophisticated for such an idea. "Forget community," say some in imperious tones. "What about my personal space? my personal goals?" others ask. Then there are those in the process of self-actualization, finding their true "self" or "inner self." Their mantra is "I ... me ... my ... mine!" The uniting cry of all these viewpoints is "Who needs community?" These are the confused voices of those overwhelmed by a sea of electronic gadgets that are supposed to make life convenient. "So what if I have no community, no neighborhood, no neighbor, no fellowship? Look at what I have: personal computers, electronic dayplanners, automatic tellers, drive-through windows for everything I need, and even virtual pets."

Cities are places where material things, often conspicuously consumed, can supplant all relationships, all community, all reality. Tragically, the present time is full of high-tech stuff, but it is empty when it comes to the human touch.

Individuals in urban areas often live fragmented existences. Is there a word from the Lord that leads out of this wilderness, a divine word that restores the fullness of humanity? Another paradox is that we can hear that word only in community. Thirst for community is built into our very being.

Why do people still seek the married life, even after multiple failures? Some never give up on love; they never tire of the desire to know another intimately and to be intimately known. They know the pain but have decided it is worth the risk. Why do so many alienated and isolated young people seek the insidious trap of gang life? Is it because they need relationships, even bad ones? Is it because they need the boundaries and the cover of community? We all need these things.

The spirit of our age questions authority. Our rebellious wills want to flatten social structures. Yet we need the structure of authority; we need authentic leaders. If we have these two attributes, together we can build genuine community. Without authority, communities disintegrate. Without authority, communities lack a center, a compass, a grounding. In communities of faith, the Gospel is authoritative. "To obtain such faith God instituted the office of the ministry, that is, provided the Gospel and the sacraments. Through these, as through means, he gives the Holy Spirit, who works faith, when and where he pleases, in those who hear the Gospel."[1]

The church, then, is a fully holy and fully human community. It is a community of mutual care, a moral community where we express and experience the theological virtues of faith, hope, and love. It is a baptized community where we truly belong to the body of Christ. At times this baptismal family has priority, especially in communities where families are divided by dysfunction or by differences. There are situations where Jesus' words ring familiar: "Do you think I came to bring peace on earth? No, I tell you, but division. From now on there will be five in one family divided against each other" (Luke 12:51–52).

> *A lot of folks in this community, even while they complain about the racial segregation, are not doing one thing about it. So that's one thing we bang on in this very mixed congregation: God has bound us together as a people, and our relationships are mediated by Christ—even if you're not acting like it. You are connected to your brother, you are connected to your sister by virtue of your connection to Christ. And that is something God has done for you. It's not something you have done for yourself. The reality of the kingdom impacts my work.—James A. Wetzstein*

The consequences of not building an authentic community in Christ are obvious to the local urban congregation: a declining and aging member base, financial instability that can lead to insolvency, a decline of prophetic credibility in the community, a weak-kneed witness, a muted voice. But this sickness is not unto death. God is powerful, and through the Spirit, he renews those congregations that in repentance and faith seek to carry out their Gospel commission.

Our community finds its unity and togetherness under the Fatherhood of God. We find our fullness in a real sisterhood and brotherhood with Jesus. Of course, we didn't find anything. We are the found ones, rescued from the exhaustion of our human journeys by the seeking Spirit of God, who never stops searching for the lost.

" 'For this is what the Sovereign LORD says: I myself will search for my sheep and look after them. As a shepherd looks after his scattered flock when he is with them, so will I look after my sheep. I will rescue them from all the places where they were scattered on a day of clouds and darkness. ... I will bring them into their own land. I will pasture them on the mountains of Israel, in the ravines and in all the settlements in the land. I will tend them in a good pasture, and the mountain heights of Israel will be their grazing land. There they will lie down in good grazing land, and there they will feed in a rich pasture on the mountains of Israel. I myself will tend my sheep and have them lie down, declares the Sovereign LORD. I will search for the lost and bring back the strays. I will bind up the injured and strengthen the weak, but the sleek and the strong I will destroy. I will shepherd the flock with justice.' "
Ezekiel 34:11–16

The Spirit who calls us by the Gospel and unites us as one body in the one saving faith is the same Spirit who seeks the lost. The challenge for urban ministry is to make churches bases for rescue and recovery missions, places where wounds are healed, souls are satisfied, and broken spirits are made whole. God calls churches to be places where goodness and kindness are shared, places where his grace in Christ and joy in the Holy Spirit abound. Churches are the environment of authentic Christian community.

Christ and Cries of Crime

The image of the city as a repository of violent crime is not new. Dr. Mark Looker teaches a course on urban perspectives at Concordia College, Ann Arbor, Mich. His students study "London: A Poem" by the 18th-century British poet Samuel Johnson. Johnson's piece is a recasting of a work by the second-century Roman writer Juvenal.

London: A Poem

by Samuel Johnson

Prepare for death, if here at night you roam,
And sign your will before you sup from home.
Some fiery fop, with new commission vain,
Who sleeps on brambles till he kills his man;
Some frolick drunkard, reeling from a feast,
Provokes a broil, and stabs you for a jest.
Yet ev'n these heroes, mischievously gay,
Lords of the street, and terrors of the way;
Flush'd as they are with folly, youth, and wine,
Their prudent insults to the poor confine;
Afar they mark the flambeau's bright approach,
And shun the shining train, and golden coach:
In vain, these dangers past, your doors you close,
And hope the balmy blessings of repose:
Cruel with guilt, and daring with despair,
The midnight murd'rer bursts the faithless bar;
Invades the sacred hour of silent rest,
And plants, unseen, a dagger in your breast.[2]

Whether Rome or London or Brooklyn, cities always have been dangerous places.

The section of Brooklyn that I am in is a neighbor-hood called East New York. It is an area of high crime. It has the highest crime statistics in all of the

city, mostly because it is the largest precinct but also
because it is one of the most violent. There are drugs
and lots of prostitution.—Steven Marsh

Crime often takes on racial overtones. Per capita, blacks are convicted of more violent crime than any other ethnic group. Currently, there are more black males incarcerated than there are in college. Nearly 50 percent of those behind U.S. prison bars are Americans of African descent. Hispanics also are disproportionately represented in prisons. But these facts tell only part of the story. They miss another tragic statistic that should not be overlooked: African American males are most often the victims of violence. Guns kill more kids in the cities—black, white, and Hispanic—than any disease or accident. Some childhood diseases have been all but eradicated, but the Centers for Disease Control in Atlanta, Geo., has identified teenage homicide as an epidemic. Boys and girls are becoming involved in violence at younger and younger ages, according to U. S. Attorney General Janet Reno. While crime rates on the whole may be declining, youth crime is rising. This trend, like so many others, appears first and most alarmingly in the cities.

Inner cities often serve as a microcosm for the nation—a barometer of our common future. Christian families are not immune to the threat of or the participation in violent crime. Yet there is a strange silence on the part of many churches that could speak out for God's pro-life indictment of violent thoughts, words, and deeds. As Martin Luther states in his explanation of the Fifth Commandment: "We must not kill, either by hand, heart, or word, by signs or gestures, or by aiding and abetting."[3]

A Pastor's Emergency

I have been a direct victim of violence only once in my life. I say "direct victim" because as Martin Luther King Jr. said, we are all united by life on this earth. Actions that directly affect one person, indirectly affect us all.[4] We are all *indirectly* affected by violence, especially because we have been claimed as heirs in Christ's kingdom. Heirs share. We cannot say, "The inner city is not my problem." When one part of the body suffers or is hurt, we all suffer and are hurt (1 Corinthians 12:26).

I did all I could on that day in August 1992. I have no lingering bitterness in my heart, though I live with an occasional nightmare. I had taken a group of young people from the church to the Erie County Fair in suburban Buffalo, New York. Most people come home from the fair with stuffed animals and cotton candy. I didn't go home for a week. I spent the time in the hospital recovering from a torn retina, a fractured eye socket, a cracked nose, and a major concussion.

Several young people I was chaperoning met up with several other young people. They exchanged words—not-so-nice words. The other young people, my group soon learned, were with a not-so-nice gang. It was a not-so-smart decision to tangle at the fair.

By the time I arrived on the scene, the verbal altercation was on the brink of a major scuffle. As pastor, I felt obligated to intervene. As I introduced myself, I emphasized my official, public status as a minister. I knew I was in trouble when the response was "We don't care if you're God Almighty!" That young man meant what he said. The melee began. I faced a pastoral emergency of the most personal type. Thank God no one in my group was hurt. In truth, I took their place, a vicarious victim.

Simply and precisely, this group of young people did not care. They had not learned the habit of caring. They could not possibly have cared for me, for their own lives, for their future, or even for that present moment. Christians should never be shocked by the paucity of compassion around us. Born into sin, humanity must be socialized—or better yet, catechized—into caring.

Communities of faith are where caring is learned. Jesus is the master caregiver. He felt it viscerally, at the deepest level of his being. He saw the harassed and helpless crowds, aimlessly wandering like sheep without a shepherd (Matthew 9:36). Effective urban leaders urgently preach with Christlike pastoral sensitivity. These are times of pastoral emergency. Pulpits can be places for administering the first-aid care of the Gospel of Jesus Christ.

We are black, and we are living in a society that is
hostile. And many are struggling to deal with this
subject. I think it is necessary to [preach] in the terms
that the black community can understand. Many of
the members have been victims of the violence, police
pressure, and so forth.—Frazier N. Odom

Places of Grace and Peace

Jesus Christ is the peace of the city. The biblical idea of peace means much more than an absence of conflict or a cessation of hostilities. God's peace, his holy shalom, is a presence, a wholeness, a discovery of that incomprehensible reconciliation that only he can grant. And he does grant it. His peace heals all broken relationships—vertically, between God and humanity, and horizontally, between sisters and brothers. Every destructive distinction between people is overcome by God's presence of peace.

There is much that breaks and bruises relationships in the city. The intense pace of life exacerbates conflict. The diminishing resources stretch patience, incite anxiety, and heighten stress.

Many urban neighborhoods are powder kegs waiting to explode. They need healing, reconciliation, and peace. Isaiah points toward the Great Day when "no longer will violence be heard in your land, nor ruin or destruction within your borders" (Isaiah 60:18). An African American spiritual says:

There is a balm in Gilead to make the wounded whole;
There is a balm in Gilead to heal the sin-sick soul.[5]

Urban preaching supplies the balm, the salve, for violence-weary people. It is the Good News of Jesus.

"Urban ministry" has to do with the Gospel on the
streets. It has to do with persons. It has to do with

*problems. It has to do with real-life situations. When
Jesus taught and preached, it was never abstract; it
was almost always concrete and real. When he talked
about wheat that yielded forty, sixty, and one hundred fold, his hearers knew what he was talking
about. Or if he talked about fish and fishing, they
knew what he was talking about. Our images are
different. Ours are the images of the street, the
images of the game, the images of drugs, the images
of addiction. These are the things in which people's
lives are shaped and molded today. They raise crucial
questions, and our answers have to be cast in terms
that people understand. If the Gospel doesn't move
into their vocabulary and their life experiences, you
are talking some other language. Urban images are
just that: the images in our neighborhood at a given
time. They have to do with hairstyles. They have to do
with how you wear your pants. They have to do with
things we laugh at, things we touch. I want the people
of the congregation to be "in" the sermon. They find
themselves in the sermon and can begin to see exactly
what was going on in Jesus' time too. When Jesus
taught people, they could find themselves in what he
was teaching.—John R. Cochran*

Paul Laurence Dunbar's classic poetic image of the caged bird
emerges as a powerful metaphor for urban preaching. (Maya
Angelou's *I Know Why the Caged Bird Sings* is better known than
the poem that inspired its title.) The image of the singing caged
bird also shapes the way urban pastors often view their ministry.

*I think that some of the images within the urban
community are that we are trapped and we feel
caged. They're similar to those of the Old Testament*

Scriptures. We also feel kind of trapped or bound by some other force. There are all kinds of forces at work in our community. The drug scene makes some people feel trapped and hopeless.—Donald E. Anthony

When we start looking at the context and the story and [when we start] understanding the pain and the grief and the agony of life and also the blessing of life and the joy of life amidst the pain, the paradoxical language that is expressed is in metaphors out of the black experience, for example, Maya Angelou's I Know Why the Caged Bird Sings.—*Joseph Donnella*

Birds of paradise is an image that stays on my mind. I used that image in a funeral sermon for a homeless man. A broken-winged bird cannot fly; that's a powerful picture. The reality of humanity wallowing in the sin and pain of the world is a picture that I often use in my preaching. As I walk along in my community—I live on the strip where the prostitutes are—I see a lot of pain, a lot of sin, a lot of wallowing in a caged world. I see a lot of people who just don't know how to get out. The church is really a place they can come to be healed ... or to be touched. We are a beacon. The church needs to be a beacon for those who are looking for a way out. And so the brokenness that we experience, I think, is a main image that I use, relating it always to the cross.—Steven Marsh

Sympathy

by Paul Laurence Dunbar

I know what the caged bird feels, alas!
When the sun is bright on the upland slopes;
When the wind stirs soft through the springing grass,
And the river flows like a stream of glass;
When the first bird sings and the first bud opes,
And the faint perfume from its chalice steals—
I know what the caged bird feels!

I know why the caged bird beats his wing
Till its blood is red on the cruel bars;
For he must fly back to his perch and cling
When he fain would be on the bough a-swing;
And a pain still throbs in the old, old scars
And they pulse again with a keener sting—
I know why he beats his wing!

I know why the caged bird sings, ah me,
When his wing is bruised and his bosom sore,—
When he beats his bars and he would be free;
It is not a carol of joy or glee,
But a prayer that he sends from his heart's deep core,
But a plea, that upward to Heaven he flings—
I know why the caged bird sings![6]

Just Words

If preaching were a sacrament, words would be the physical element—or perhaps transphysical element because words obviously have no physical property. Languages are systems of signs that express meaning. That meaning is conveyed in a variety of ways: the organization of words, the momentum of experience brought to the conversation by the speaker and the hearer, and the actual choice of words.

Meeting the challenge of the vernacular in urban settings is a high and holy task. Preaching often is defined by imagination and narration, by a sense of spontaneity in the encounter with the Word. The structure of the urban sermon is not loose or unorganized; it is free and freeing. The rhythm and the cadence more closely resemble the blues or jazz than baroque or classical music. As in jazz, artists of the Word must find their own voice—in this case, a preaching voice. This is achieved by thoroughly researching the text and rehearsing how the message will be "done." In Gerhard Forde's model, the art of preaching is a "doing" of the text to the hearers. This preaching is polished in the pastor's study and the pulpit. Preachers perfect their form so they may be free to improvise. The best improvisation is a "planned spontaneity."

As in jazz, preaching that is close to the streets specializes in syncopated sounds, in call-and-response dialog, in a sacred exchange that is flexible to the hearers' responses of prayer, praise, and thanksgiving. The congregation delights in hearing the grace of God in Christ Jesus. The preacher's words meet with joy. The words are metered and measured by thumping floorboards, tapping toes, and clapping hands. Urban preachers whisper, shout, chant, and may even rap their way through the message.

Sticks and Stones

The childhood phrase "Sticks and stones may break my bones, but words will never hurt me" is an outright lie. Solomon, the sage of the Old Testament, had it right: "The tongue has the power of life and death" (Proverbs 18:21). Words can cut; words can kill. Whoever has been the target of hateful put-downs by those who think they are superior knows how words can pierce like the thrust of a sword. Whoever has been the target of a placard such as "For Whites Only"; whoever has heard the muted voice of a hiring manager say, "It's a man's job" knows what words can do. But words also can help and heal. Gospel words—especially justification—bring life.

If you want to talk about Lutheran theology, you have to begin with justification. And when you talk about justification by grace, you talk about people being justified without condition. A welcome word in the urban context is forgiveness. We work over and over with people, many of whom have failed in this and failed in that, stumbled with this and stumbled

*with that. The word is [that] "You're okay" and that
"You're forgiven. Let's go ahead. Christ forgives—he
justifies. You move ahead from right here. Christ
takes you right where you are; now let's go."
Justification is a powerful, renewing word in this
place. It is the word of forgiveness. It is the word of
future. It is a word that says, "Christ accepts you."—
John R. Cochran*

The cornerstone of Lutheran theology is the doctrine of justification. Our search for an image that speaks God's Word to God's people who dwell in a diverse urban cultural setting is formed by this hallmark doctrine. Any image worth employing must not swerve or veer from the main emphasis of the Bible, the doctrine of how sinners are made right with God through Jesus Christ. Rudolph Blank advises the use of this sort of epistemological filter: "Justification by faith is the hermeneutical key for understanding liberation or any other major Biblical concept."[1] Thus, we always proceed in our search for images to speak God's grace in the city through the lens of justification terminology.

*One of the reasons that I feel very comfortable
remaining a Lutheran—Lutheran Church—
Missouri Synod, even—is that our theology, our doctrine, stresses the grace element, how the grace of God
in Christ releases us.—Donald E. Anthony*

Fundamentalism's Words

"We live according to the Bible, word for word, verse by verse. That's God's blueprint for human success." Sentiments such as these sound good, but they greatly overstate how we relate to the Word and to the world. These perspectives abound in urban areas. Chaos, rapid change, and uncertainty often lead to an affection for fundamentalist forms of Christianity.

But the primary epistemological problem with such an approach lies in its claim not to have presuppositions. It's like having a bucket without a bottom. Everyone has a starting point from which they interpret the Bible. In the Christian community, everyone begins with some essential, biblically based (or related) presuppositions. For Lutherans, the presuppositions that shape our view are the Latin *solas*: grace, Christ, faith, and Scripture alone. Another presupposition is the paradoxical stereophonic sound of God's Word to humans: Law and Gospel. Finally, we see Scripture's *cantus firmus,* its bedrock doctrine, justification, or how the sinner is made right with God through Jesus Christ.

Evangelical Lutheran words always are accompanied with the evangelical use of the sacraments. The Lord's Supper is the visible word, conferring the forgiveness it promises in the real presence of Jesus Christ in bread and wine. Likewise, Baptism has the command and promise of Christ. His grace works through water and the Word. These are signs that communicate as forcefully as the words spoken from the pulpit or lectern.

Metaphors

Metaphors are tools of speech. They vary in how directly they correlate to truth. But in and of themselves, metaphors are not meant to bear truth or falsehood. As communication devices, metaphors elucidate; they make truth more clear.

> Metaphor is the richest and most powerful of all the rhetorical devices. Perhaps Aristotle's classic definition is a good place to begin: "The application of an alien name by transference." In other words, a term belonging somewhere else is used in an unusual context, as when we say, "Sherry is a rose," "Time is a thief," or as when the death of a man on a cross is called a victory.

Yet a metaphor is more than mere "word games," (
and certainly not an abuse of language, as some people think. It used to be a fairly common viewpoint
that a metaphor was basically a lie. Saying, for example, that a "cross" is a "victory" is a lie, an untruth,
since we all know that a cross literally is not a victory. It is a bloody and horrible death and a defeat.
One still often hears this disparagement of these
devices as "merely rhetorical," or "merely metaphorical," as opposed to what is literal and real.

However, metaphor is necessary for the advancement of knowledge.[2]

Biblical metaphors, so rich and so varied, set the parameters
for the preaching task as the *missio Dei* is presented from urban pulpits. "The Scriptures heap such descriptive synonyms on top of
each other, and Christian witness can be more effectively communicated if the believer is familiar with these synonyms for salvation
and is conscious of the possibility of finding others in contemporary culture."[3]

An extended metaphor—a story—may be used in preaching
to capture a truth and convey it within a context. Stories as
metaphors are best used when they are seen as servants of the
Gospel, not equals with or masters of the Gospel.

> *The Gospel must predominate. Folks need to hear*
> *that Jesus suffered, bled, died, and was resurrected*
> *again—all to save us from our sins.—Victor J. Belton*

There are clear connections that readily link the Lutheran tradition to current perspectives on urban preaching. Often, preaching is the prime focus of urban worship, especially where liturgical
symbols, signs, gestures, and actions are not held in high regard.
Preaching is viewed as a direct, clear word from the Lord. The
preacher's voice has authority. "Talkin' the talk" carries signifi-

cance. Luther's axiom that the church is the "mouth house" of God should find a warm welcome in the city.

> *Justification by faith is appropriate for the urban scene, especially where you have a lot of different cultures. Among urban people in particular, the tension creates a lot of individuals who try to justify themselves and raise themselves up.—Carlos Hernandez*

Proclaiming a universal, objective justification is nonnegotiable. The central *kerygma*—that Christ died for all irrespective of status or background or social condition—is the church's lifeline. Preaching the Gospel moves us toward a community in which all cultures are respected, all people are regarded as worthwhile, and all nations have value because God so loved the whole cosmos that He gave His only Son as the Savior. This "theological personalism"—the truth that all people and cultures, by virtue of their creation by God and the objective reconciliation achieved by Christ, are the proper focus of the Church's mission—is critical to the city. Everyone needs to hear the Law and Gospel; God desires salvation of every single mother and child, every restless young man roaming urban streets. It's God's will—no one is to be lost!

> *Jesus died for all. We must continue lifting up that truth. He died for that dirty one lying on the side of the street that has binged all night long. You may not like him; he may be dirty and he may be smelly, but Jesus died for him. You see that poor person on the corner begging for money. It may be inconvenient for you, but Jesus died for him. You think of a person who has been abused in her family, and even though you may not know it, she is sitting in church beside you every Sunday. Jesus died for her. We have handicapped folks that come in wheelchairs. Sometimes they block the aisles or do some other things that may not*

be comfortable for the congregation, but they belong in this house. Jesus died for them. You never know when Jesus is going to lift one of them up. We have folks that come that are mentally handicapped or challenged, and we tell them to keep it down and not make a lot of noise. But we want them in the house because Jesus died for them. All those hungry folks, homeless folks, and those folks in high rises, and those folks in tenements, those rich folks and poor folks— Jesus died for each and every one. So we make no distinction as we go about sharing the Gospel in the city.—*Victor J. Belton*

Countering Counterfeit
Liberation

Lutherans who preach within a Confessional sphere know that there never can be a purely political solution to any human problem. Because we are beset by sin and chained to irreversible depravity, we cannot gain genuine freedom by putting into place human measures. What the Holy Spirit works is not a program, not a political campaign, not a social platform. It is a transformation through the Gospel. What ails urban communities, like all others, falls within the scope of theology, not ideology. The *kerygma* of the Church is unique, but it is also ideally suited to the world's dilemmas and difficulties. The Gospel brings true liberation for enslaved humankind.

Blatant social disparity in cities around the world has produced the churchly hermeneutic and praxis known as liberation theology. Lutherans contend that the distinction between the kingdoms of grace and power are blurred by strict—some would say radical—liberation theologians. Liberation theology dissolves the tension of God's right and left hands in the world. It also flattens the paradox of eschatological life—"here and now" yet also "then and there"—the "not yet" of God's redemptive work. Liberation theology dispenses with the distinction between the kingdoms: the one not of this world and the one of this world, which in the interim remains under enemy control. Liberation theology shortens the hope for the future kingdom and presents, instead, a radical contemporaneity. It truncates history so God's kingdom is preached as an immanent kingdom where justice rules the earth today.

> *The two kingdoms fits perfectly because of the different arenas in which we live and the many responsibilities that we have: responsibilities within family, within the congregation, within the neighborhood, within the political arena, and so on. The same standards do not pertain in these different contexts.—John R. Cochran*

To embrace the gift of culture and variety also means to accept the limitations that culture brings to our world. Culture itself is human and, therefore, imperfect. Though some may claim otherwise, culture must be judged. Urban pulpits, therefore, proclaim above all a biblical understanding of culture.

> *It's easy to admire Luther's understanding of the two kingdoms. There is also no way of being a responsible citizen and living responsibly as a citizen in the world if you don't understand how the world operates. The world operates in a way that is different from the way the church operates. So we spend a lot of time talking about our place as citizens in this culture as well. Live out your calling where God has placed you, to the glory of God.—James A. Wetzstein*

An Idea Whose Time Is Past

When preachers allow their messages to veer into discussions about a human heaven, such talk cannot bear a healthy harvest. Any attempt to construct an earthly utopia apart from Christ, whether from the left or the right, is prone to despotism. Jürgen Moltmann is one such thinker. His heaven is not "above," existing in transcendence, it is "ahead," approaching from the future. His christological formulations are steeped in the language of liberation: "The crucified God is in fact a stateless and classless God. ... He is the God of the poor, the oppressed and the humiliated. The rule of Christ who was crucified for political reasons can only be extended through liberation from forms of rule which make men servile and apathetic and the political religions which give them stability."[1]

Another shade of liberation theology emphasizes economics. Variations of Marxism are the philosophy of choice for Cornel West. He is widely recognized as an articulate proponent of how Christianity and progressive Marxism can be merged—in his view, *must* be merged—as a tool to end oppression. He contends that his brand of revolutionary Christianity must include Marxist social theory and political praxis, which also acts to liberate God's chosen people from the experience of victimization at the hands of free-market capitalists. West supposes that such a praxis must stand within the Christian tradition, in particular the African American Christian experience with its commitment to both individuality and community.[2]

Not only are there many philosophical questions about the soundness of the presuppositions of liberation theology, there is scant evidence for its effectiveness in urban settings. Even a theologian sympathetic to the movement, James H. Harris, concedes that black theology has failed to reach those to whom it was intended to bring liberty.[3] Harris is not referring to the need of urban blacks and Hispanics for a culturally informed theology; rather he is speaking of that branch of liberation theology called black theology.

Liberation theology has suffered a loss of momentum. Many mourn the apparent demise of the radical edge of the civil rights movement. The purpose of movements is to move and to motivate. When any movement is more concerned about its loss of momentum than it is about the cause that drew it together or the issue that sparked its response, these are sure signs that the association or the idea has outlived its usefulness. Movements are meant to lead people forward. Liberation theology has not done that effectively in the city, despite its noble motives.

The experience of racism has contributed to a sociological and psychological phenomenon expressed as "victimization." When self-esteem is tied so tightly to the race experience, individuals can develop an unhealthy, even harmful, preoccupation with race. Communities, too, can suffer from corporate victimization. The Gospel of Jesus Christ is the answer—especially when it is applied contextually by preaching the metaphors appropriate for the community.

> *My preaching is that God loves you, that God did not make a mistake with you, regardless of what racists and others say. You are God's, and he has placed you where he needs you. I preach with all of my heart that God knows exactly where you are and God put you right here this morning. I want to get at the race problem in terms of Law and Gospel.—Frazier N. Odom*

Victory Snatched from Defeat

Too much of urban life is defeat. Daily existence is eked out in tired streets or spent cities. Children, whose futures should be full of hope, feel the weight of failure and destruction. Perhaps most tragically, in many urban neighborhoods senior citizens cower in fear as prisoners of their own homes.

As a vicar in Buffalo, New York, I conducted the funeral of Terry Crawford. A man of dignity and honor, Terry was a jazz musician from the glory days of this western New York city's version of the Harlem Renaissance. He lived to be a nonagenarian only to have his proud life snuffed out by a cowardly punk. First, the young man robbed Terry's apartment. Then he mercilessly threw the ailing and frail man down the back flight of steps, killing him, before fleeing with a few dollars and trinkets. During the sermon, in a twist on the basic Lutheran question, I asked, "What does this *life* mean?" I had one answer, "Absolutely nothing!"

Nowhere in North America is the creeping threat of meaninglessness more profound than in our urban communities. Clearly, this is out of sync with God's plan. The poet laureate of Lutheranism, Martin Franzmann, wrote with power about the transformative effect of God's Word.

> O God, O Lord of heav'n and earth
> Your living finger never wrote
> That life should be an aimless mote,
> A deathward drift from futile birth.
> Your Word meant life triumphant hurled
> In splendor through your broken world,
> since light awoke and life began
> You made for us a holy plan.[4]

God provides a triumphant answer for the Terrys of this world. The sacred Scriptures promise much more than defeat and doom as final destiny. The urban reality around us is a perversion of the divine design. God's Word means life. That Word transforms and gives meaning to lives. It is incarnate in Christ, recorded in the Bible, visible in the bread and wine of the Eucharist and in the water of Baptism.

> *Sometimes our preaching seems contradictory, but in fact those kinds of evocative symbols in language are true to our experience as a community, as African Americans, and as Africans. We use those kinds of symbols and we start talking about God, not*

*in abstraction, but God in the metaphorical, analog-
ical language of the Scriptures.—Joseph Donnella*

Setting the Captives Free

Much scholarly literature in the study of African American
and Latino history casts oppression/liberation as the central dialectic. These groups have been oppressed; their search for freedom has
defined their collective consciousness. Though valid for historical
analysis, especially in respect to slavery and the discrimination
endured by minorities in America, it is not apparent that scholarship actually has brought about change. Is it useful today—helpful
to urban communities—to focus on the victimization of the past?

According to Shelby Steele, group identity that concentrates
on suffering leads to spiritual shackles and a pathological sense of
inferiority.[5] It is ironic that the scapegoat for every individual or
community challenge becomes the experience of victimhood. The
victims victimize themselves.

> *As a child growing up in urban Houston, we lived
> in the shadow of a Lutheran congregation that would
> not accept Mexicans. So the Texas District started a
> Mexican mission about three or four blocks from us.
> The feeling conveyed here was that we were second
> class. But justification by grace says in no way are
> you second class, no way are you any less than anyone
> else.—Carlos Hernandez*

A biblical category that forcefully and clearly speaks to the
challenges of life in urban America is victory. A victory-filled vocabulary in the pulpit could strike at the heart of the existential condition in urban culture in a way that is true to social, economic, and
spiritual reality yet congruent with the imagery of the Scriptures.
Many who live in urban areas suffer from *angst,* a deep feeling of

inferiority, of failure. When this angst is coupled with hopelessness, the result is chronic despair. There is an urgent need to speak the Gospel in a liberating tone but without the entrapping language of victimology evident in liberation theology.

The corrupt environment of the city, the corrupted nature of humanity, and the corrupting forces of evil have a corrosive effect on cities. Many people struggle with a deep psychological sense of defeat that, if unchecked, can develop into a cycle of defeat. Among racial and ethnic minorities, this often takes the shape of an exaggerated awareness of inferiority. To compensate for a system that leaves self-image corrupted, an individual may choose options that appear to alleviate that feeling of worthlessness but in fact lead to greater dependency or greater debt or greater mental depression or even death. Justification-as-victory can become the uniquely Lutheran doctrinal contribution to urban preaching. It truly can bring life through the preacher's words.

> *God declares us saved through Christ's suffering,*
> *death, and resurrection. "Not with gold or silver,"*
> *Luther says in the explanation to the Second Article,*
> *"but with His holy, precious blood and with His inno-*
> *cent suffering and death." It's like wow! A load is*
> *lifted from people's shoulders.—Carlos Hernandez*

To this malady of inferiority, the primary word of Gospel in preaching and pastoral care is Christ's victory. Gerhard Aho identifies three Law and Gospel correlations: Guilt-Forgiveness, Defeat-Victory, and Obedience-Power. On the Defeat-Victory dialectic, Aho writes: "The Law not only accuses but exposes. It describes the predicament we human beings are in because of sin. ... Here the stress is on the horizontal rather than on the vertical dimension."[6]

Gospel Power

I've been spending a lot of time studying Lutheran Christology, like Chemnitz, and trying to understand it apart from Aristotelian scholastic teaching. I've been well rewarded because I've gained a lot of insight and appreciation for a distinctly Lutheran Christology. The Gospel is the righteousness of God. As St. Paul says: "The power of God for the salvation of everyone who believes." People need that power. People want to be connected to that power.—Doyle J. Theimer

Such "empowering" is wrapped up in the metaphor of victory. The preacher nobly directs the hearer toward the spiritual resources that Christ has supplied to his people. This is the source of strength that leads to freedom because, as a rule, people cannot be genuinely free as long as they depend on other human beings for their deliverance. Deliverance is found only in Christ. We are bathed—though Baptism—into the freedom that makes us free indeed.

Luther talks about the significance of Baptism with water. In Baptism, we find our hope; the old self is drowned daily through repentance and forgiveness, and the new person rises daily. So even though we may feel put down by others, by our own selves, [by] our own guilt, by the devil's accusing finger, in that repentance and forgiveness—[a] return to our Baptism—a new person arises.—Carlos Hernandez

What to Watch with Metaphors

There are, however, some cautions to consider when metaphors, metaphoric language, and synonyms are employed for the Gospel, especially if one particular metaphor is used repeatedly or exclusively.

First, metaphorical language can lead to relativism. Many postmodern theologians claim that human language is inadequate for communication about God; therefore, metaphors *must* be used. This theory, in its fascination with perspective and interpretation, undermines authoritative truth. In some academic fields, language is the ultimate tool, not the truth that language conveys. Such humanistic overconfidence in perspective and language is not the preacher's reason to use metaphors. Rightly used, metaphors are not simply a matter of language in which everyone has the right to a point of view, opinion, approach, and interpretation. (Television talk shows represent the most absurd popularization of this phenomena.) Rather, metaphors speak the same singular truth from varying biblically based angles.

A second caution when using metaphors of justification in preaching would be to avoid mixing these metaphors. If an image is introduced, it is preached most intelligibly when it is resolved. Legal or forensic language about justification is one category of metaphor. Other metaphors also express the vitality and capacity of the Gospel to connect with human life.[7] As Joseph Sittler has warned: "It is the task of theology to keep categories clean, to explicate the faith of the church in categories which are inwardly fashioned by the particularity of the events and affirmations which are constitutive of the community of the people of God."[8]

Lutherans seem comfortable speaking the language of guilt/forgiveness. This paradigm is sometimes preferred at the expense of other available, powerful, and poignant metaphors. At other times, this metaphor is forced onto biblical models for describing what Christ has done for humanity. Have Lutherans been too rigidly defined by a forensic model of justification? Has the prevailing model of sin/guilt predictably followed by preaching forgiveness been tied too tightly to Lutheran identity? Is this pre-eminent metaphor sometimes even an obstacle for transcultural mission? These are essential questions with which the church, including the urban church, must wrestle.

Ross Aden offers these poignant observations:

> The Lutheran theologian Gerhard O. Forde blames the forensic metaphor itself for our problems. According to Forde, both traditional Lutheranism and traditional Catholicism are caught in the same "legal scheme." The one side guards the purity of the doctrine of grace but tends to make salvation into something unreal; while the other side insists that justification must involve transformation but tends to compromise the gracefulness of God's declaration of righteousness in Christ by requiring its realization in a holy life. Both sides of the impasse are controlled by the fundamental metaphor of the divine law court, a metaphor which fails at the critical point because it cannot answer the very question of how the work of Christ changes the sinner. Forde holds that the forensic metaphor must no longer be allowed to dominate our theology but that it should be balanced by another metaphor.[9]

The forensic metaphor's dominance of the urban pulpit is not to be underestimated. Some Lutheran theologians have gone so far as to state that without direct preaching about forgiveness of sins and the imputation of righteousness using a forensic model there is no preaching of justification. "Any deviation from this model buries Christ, burdens consciences, and takes away the comfort of the Gospel."[10] But this likely says more than Scripture and the Confessions intend. Although forensic language and imagery dominate, such language should not exclude other biblical motifs.

Robert Jensen bemoans the typical "Lutheran" sermon. First, we hear "an analysis of some aspect of fallen human life, often very well done. Then will come the 'gospel'-part: 'To be sure, we must recognize that we cannot by our own reason or strength do differently. Never mind, for Jesus' sake God loves you anyway.' "[11] If Jensen's caricature is close to accurate, the preaching of justification has devolved significantly from Luther's evangelical ideal.

The typical Lutheran preaching of the Law—which targets guilt, sin, and shame—may not be effective in most urban settings. It may not connect with African Americans because of the more immediate—even concrete—issues of survival.

> *People in urban contexts often are seeking survival at any cost. And that's the way I look at many of our people: They're seeking survival. But we have the all-powerful, proven solution in the Word of God.—*
> *Ulmer Marshall Jr.*

Shelby Steele has noted that the essence of white anxiety is guilt—not a debilitating, crushing anguish, but more a sense of racial vulnerability. Steele makes the point that many blacks, who possess a "victim-focused identity," can appeal to white guilt and, in this area of racial vulnerability, demand reparations and redress.[12] The contrasting vulnerability of blacks is, according to Steele, the "hidden inferiority anxiety."[13] Although Steele is analyzing racial and social matters, could there be a corresponding and similar anxiety to which the doctrine of justification might be addressed?

A heightened inferiority anxiety (as contrasted with guilt anxiety) does not exculpate inner-city residents from personal responsibility. Nor does it excuse people from living as moral agents, despite their natural sinful condition. But inferiority anxiety does require a shift in the preaching of the Law. Too frequently the recognition of sin for urban people includes accepting the experience of alienation, blindly embracing "hardship or persecution" (Romans 8:35) in a fatalistic manner as a predetermined destiny.

This does not accurately reflect the biblical idea of sin as a tyrant that subverts God's creative and redemptive purposes. This is a preaching of the Law, as one Lutheran theologian described it, not so much "rooted in an act of rebellion but in a fact of alienation."[14]

> *We try to give people a sense of uplift, a sense of "Even though we are in the midst of struggles, there is also victory." I guess those are two components: struggle and victory. When we talk about the struggle and victory, we also talk about the cross and resurrection. African American people need to hear a word of Christ that says, "Yes, I am along with you in terms of struggle." But they also need to hear the word of Christ, "Yes, I have won your victory." Come struggles, yet victory will out in the preached word every Sunday.—James Capers*

It's time to leave Egypt behind and march forward. We march with confidence because God goes before us, with us, and behind us. We march on because the goal is not the march itself but the destination: the Promised Land. "The suffering of the African Americans was immeasurably oppressive, but they overcame the temptation to succumb to defeatism and escapism. They overcame such challenges and persisted in hope. This was their long-term strategy."[15] Martin Luther's maxim *Unum praedica: sapientiam crucis*—Preach one thing: the wisdom of the cross—is significant to every challenge we face. If there is no preaching of the cross of Christ, then there cannot be any preaching of the victory of Christ. The resurrection power of that victory is inextricably bound up in the crucified, dying Savior.

This is the time to face the rising sun. In this light a people see and seize the opportunity. As Shelby Steele observes: "It was the emphasis on mass action in the sixties that made the victim-focused black identity a necessity. But in the nineties and beyond, when racial advancement will come only through a multitude of individual advancements, this form of identity inadvertently adds itself to the forces that hold us back."[16] That journey cannot be made without faith in a Christian sense.

Would victory be a metaphor Martin Luther might employ? Herman Steumpfle writes: "Luther can speak of the human condition in terms other than guilt."[17] Indeed, for Luther and many others the cross was the site of a battle, a "magnificent duel," a cosmic struggle in which Christ invaded the realm of the devil to defeat him forever. *Iesous Christos is Christus Victor.* Jaroslav Pelikan summarizes that the cross is "the sign of God's invasion of enemy territory and of the 'wondrous battle [*mirabile duellum*]' by which Jesus Christ had accomplished the salvation of the human race."[18] Yet the strength of this metaphor exposes a potential weakness: The emphasis on the utter defeat of demonic powers threatens to overshadow the vicarious satisfaction. Jesus died in our place. Our sin was on him. Not only did Christ defeat the devil, he defeated the death sentence of sin on our lives.

The big call to God's people today is to keep the faith in a world that obviously doesn't work. Everybody recognizes that there is a lot of "stuff" in this area that is dysfunctional and dying. But the Gospel creates life in our hopelessness. The Gospel is power.—James A. Wetzstein

Those people living and dying in cities for whom life consists of nothing more than "fac[ing] death all day long; ... as sheep to be slaughtered" (Romans 8:36) will appreciate the hope and power in Christ's victory. In the midst of defeat and our desultory existence, death is rendered impotent—stinger-less—by the Victor who gives "total victory" (*hypernike*). While the Law uncovers and identifies the precise lapses that spell defeat in life, the Gospel fills the gaps with victory. The word *Gospel* carries connotations of victory, in fact, the Greek word for "gospel," *euangelion,* means "good news." This particular word in the Greek signified news of a military victory or other important event in the life of the emperor.[19] This victory is not only a referential point of preaching, it is actually given in the preaching. God's Word confers and confirms what it conveys because the preacher's voice is the living voice of God (*vive vox Dei*). Preaching is more proclamation than simple communication.

The lion and the lamb were two messianic images from the Old Testament Scriptures. In some ways they are so distinctive that some thought there would be more than one Messiah. Christ is the Lamb of God who takes away the sin of the world (John 1:29), but he is also the Lion of Judah (Genesis 49:9). This lion-like Messiah is victorious as he mauls, mangles, and massacres the enemies of God (Micah 5:8). In the end, this conquering Lion rules triumphant in glory (Revelation 5:5). Urban churches can reverberate with this compelling image of a Savior who is aggressive in love, who rescues and redeems. This Jesus is no weak, wimpy, New Age Gnostic ghost of a man. He is "Judah's Lion" who "wins the strife And conquers death to give us life."[20] No one compels him to go to the execution, but he voluntarily surrenders and willingly sacrifices his life for those he loves (John 10:18).

Preaching as Celebration

If the preaching of Martin Franzmann is emblematic of Lutheran homiletics, every sermon properly "ends on a note of 'high doxology' in the declaration of the forgiving love of our Lord."[21] The high doxology of urban preaching as a whole, and in particular of preaching in the African American tradition, finds compatibility with Lutheran preaching. Such a joyous tone prefigures and anticipates the unending eschatological celebration. It also serves an earthly purpose. It is sustained praise for the battle-weary believer who, in Christ, awaits the full victory. By adding a celebrative, even festive, conclusion to preaching, urban pastors embody God's victory. "Public jubilation should not be reserved for touchdowns and home runs. Authentic gospel feasting begets its own irresistible celebration; to hold it back or inhibit it is to lose the joy itself, along with the whole message."[22]

The climactic celebration so characteristic of African American preaching can be married easily to the victory metaphor. Our pulpits then recognize God's swift, preemptive stroke in Christ that defeats everything that would ruin his people. Our pulpits announce and celebrate the victory that lies ahead: "I am coming soon" (Revelation 22:7). In Christ, the final victory is so certain that it renders all hardships and heartaches transitory, not eternal. Our kingdom focus is not a pie-in-the-sky, hyperspiritual Christianity. It is an authentic, Spirit-inspired hope. This festive preaching comes from mouths that overflow with hallelujahs and eyes that, by faith, are fixed on the cross. The cross of Jesus Christ is the central event of history. On it, our Lord "conquered the devil and gave us his promise and the Holy Spirit, so that with the help of God we, too, might conquer."[23]

Saying It in the City

What's Your Story

In African American preaching, the most visible symbol has been preachers—their storytelling style, their personal art form, and their flare for communication. As in pop culture as a whole, this passion and spontaneity is an exportable element. Especially in cities, many Anglos and Latinos expertly draw on freer, dialogical, and narrative patterns for preaching.

> *A lot of my preaching takes the form of narrative. I'm looking for angles on storytelling, in the way stories are developed. I'm also looking [at] movies, for example, [for] the ways movie directors pick up and develop themes. Scenes of restoration, scenes of hope,*

scenes of depravity—each convey striking images and
themes. The fact is the folks in the pews are watching
these movies, so you have a natural connecting point.
Fortunately or unfortunately, my sermons very rarely
make it to a manuscript. They seem to evaporate
after Sunday morning.—James A. Wetzstein

As the rise of rap music can attest, urban culture is rich in folk storytelling tradition. Rap music serves as urban "literature" in the same way graffiti often functions as urban art. (In its protest mode, graffiti is the hieroglyphics of alienation.) Rap is the Underground Railroad of communication.

In rap, a strong beat-oriented musical line forms a supporting understructure for the rhythmically spoken vocal line. Yet the primary communication remains verbal, not musical. Rap musicians, like urban preachers, speak within a cultural stream where words still possess a powerful currency. Their art is characterized by verbal wizardry. Perhaps rap music is, in some sense, a secularized and popularized version of the black preaching tradition.

When language is viewed as a tool of oppression, those who see themselves as oppressed by language sometimes manipulate the meaning of that language. They twist syntax in an attempt to make words liberating. Urban dwellers are not the first to distrust the way in which language is used. King David once plaintively pleaded with God: "Not a word from their mouth can be trusted; their heart is filled with destruction. Their throat is an open grave; with their tongue they speak deceit" (Psalm 5:9).

The youth of the inner city, often without realizing it, manipulate the rules to give words new meanings. The word *bad*, of course, may mean "good." "My nigga" might even be a designation of affection. In many ways, language is more alive and changing in the city. Thus, even in these days, preaching stands an excellent opportunity for a renewal and revival of its effectiveness, starting in the urban setting.

Some maintain that words are no longer enough to communicate, that effective speaking requires the addition of visual aids or electronic media to keep the focus of an attention-deficit modern world. Rap music suggests otherwise. It is strongly word oriented—it is verbally driven. The speaking itself—in the case of preaching, the proclamation—still can have ritually strong and symbolic impact in urban communities.

I found it necessary to get away from the pulpit and get to where people are and to speak to the congregation. I don't want to read a text; I want to speak to people, so my sermons have assumed a different character. I knew that I had to get away from the paper and the pulpit. I find it very confining to have to preach that way again. The sermons are much more dialogical now. In the last 25 years, it has never been unusual for a conversation to occur in the congregation during the sermon. Beware of any rhetorical questions because someone will surely answer. The whole experience of preaching in this context is very alive. People not only listen but answer.—John R. Cochran

Another clear point of connection between Lutheran theology and urban preaching is the sense of *Deus locutus* in the act of preaching. That is, it is God who is speaking. Martin Luther clearly articulated that in the preaching, in the absolving, in the blessing, and in other such public, pastoral acts, God is speaking through the preacher. Lowell Green further connects the relationship between the messenger and God's message:

According to the Sacred Scriptures and the Lutheran Confessions, God saves sinners through the *media salutis,* "instruments of salvation," or means of grace. When the pastor preaches properly, the sermon is the Word of God; when he baptizes, it is Christ who baptizes through his agency; when he forgives or retains sin, it is Christ himself who absolves through the pastor's mouth; when he hands out the consecrated elements, it is Christ himself who is present and bestows his body and blood in the sacrament.[1]

The preacher's voice is heard as the very voice of God—*vive vox Dei.*

Sing a New Song

Blues, rock, reggae, salsa, jazz, grunge, and hip hop. The rhythms of the city are syncopated and pulsating sounds. Sometimes this music is like life—cacophonous, clashing, clanging. These sounds often reflect the intense rhythms and competing beats that characterize the city.

Yet the Holy Spirit is also at work with a new song. He produces faith. Lives are transformed, hope is renewed, forgiveness is spread widely, and families are restored. The Word of God's Good News in Jesus Christ is instrumental. Although the pattern of social and spiritual pain is repeated in many places in America, the abundance of churches and Gospel preachers provides hope. The urban landscape is dotted with these churches, these "preaching houses." While many other noble institutions have decayed in the core cities of America, the Christian church has remained a mainstay of urban culture. Property values may have declined, businesses and schools may have disappeared, but congregational ministries have endured. In large part, this is because of preaching. Preaching is the sound of the city. It is a voice that gives meaning to modern urban life.

Three Voices
from the City

A Cross, a Defeat, and a Victory

JOHN NUNES

Based on Romans 8:31–37, this sermon illustrates the defeat of city life interpreted and transformed by Christ's victory on the cross.

"With these super-ordinary gym shoes on your ordinary feet," claims the hyped-up, slickly produced TV ad, "you'll run faster, jump higher, play better, perform stronger, and last longer than your competitors."

That's the kind of victory you are guaranteed for $200 of leather, rubber, and man-made parts expertly stitched and glued together and laced up on even your below-average feet. People pay high prices to win.

Secretly, we're all somewhat sick, stricken with a superstar syndrome. Nobody likes losing, and nobody likes a loser.

If we're that loser, we can even hate ourselves. Forget the worse-than-death fate of finishing last; few people remember who won the bronze or silver. Bridesmaids stand in the shadows of the bride. Runners-up are disregarded. The winner's circle is the spotlight. That's the only place to be.

Consider my favorite football team, the Buffalo Bills, the only football team in the history of the NFL good enough to make it to four consecutive Super Bowls, and I guess you could say the only team bad enough to lose all four. So no matter how many great games they won to get there, they seem destined to be the butt of bad jokes such as: Do you know what the B-I-L-L-S of Buffalo Bills stands for? It means "Boy, I Love Losing Superbowls."

Losing in sports is one thing. You can usually walk away. What about when you lose in life? When we look around our community, we see signs of people who can't get away from the losing side of life. Theirs is never to win, never to succeed, and never to overcome. Some have checked out of the arena of ordinary human participation. They've resigned themselves to a life of losing, and even their religion merely serves to make them feel good about losing. Their religion can indeed be an opiate, a magic emotional pill that gives them temporary relief from the pain of defeat. That, my sisters and brothers, is not Good News from God!

When people begin to live on the losing side of life, they begin to develop some strange behaviors. Like a basketball team that's so far behind that they've given up on catching up so they start fouling other players, fouling themselves right out of the game, some in our community have become so resigned to losing that we've developed some strange behaviors, some destructive and negative pathologies, some sinful ways of dealing with life.

I like the way Alan Keyes describes the problem. He was the only African American to enter the 1996 presidential race. He was the former president of Alabama A & M University. In his new book titled *Masters of the Dream* (subtitled *The Strength and Betrayal of Black America*), Keyes contends rightly, in my opinion, that black youth aren't dying or becoming pregnant at the hands of racists. African Americans are killing and abusing one another. Then Keyes asks how our ancestors could live through incredible systemic abuse to person and livelihood without self-destructing or losing their moral compass?[1]

That's what happens when you let your losing circumstances destroy your spirit. Your spirit becomes a breeding ground for sin. Jesus not only has an answer to this dilemma of defeat, Jesus is the answer. John called him the way, truth, and life.

Certainly the government has no solution. Richard John Neuhaus punctuates this point: "Since Lyndon Johnson's war on poverty, the government has spent five trillion dollars on programs allegedly helping poor people, with the result that there are more poor people in a more desperate state of dependency than thirty years ago."[2]

Occasionally, miraculously, some people break out of the cycle. Sadly, they end up the victims of ridicule. Our world is obviously designed to humble, humiliate, or even punish those who don't measure up. But sometimes it is even harder on those who do succeed. They are called race traitors. Sneered at as sellouts. Labeled as culturally unauthentic Uncle Toms or even more graphically as "house niggers." Motivated by a new sense of who they are in Jesus Christ, their faith empowers them to defy the narrow definitions of what is American and what is African American.

As Henry Louis Gates warns us: "We cannot, finally, succumb to the temptation to resurrect our own version of the Thought Police, who would determine who, and what, is 'black.' 'Mirror, Mirror on the Wall, Who's the Blackest One of All?' is a question best left behind in the sixties."[3]

Would you agree with me that there are as many different ways to be black as there are different ways to be white? Brilliance comes in many shades, styles, and flavors. Whether it's Kathleen Battle singing a Johann Sebastian Bach aria or ZZ Hill singing "Down Home Blues." Whether it's Grant Hill driving to the rim on the basketball court or Clarence Thomas rendering a decision as a member of the Supreme Court. Whether it's athlete Carl Lewis winning Olympic gold or businessman Reginald Lewis, who earned the gold for Beatrice Foods.

I don't know about you, but personally I refuse to be pigeon-holed into anybody's stereotype of black. The Gospel calls us out of pigeonholes and foxholes and puts us on the front line where we can win in the face of all of these things.

Nike is a company that makes gym shoes and many other things bearing that famous swoosh symbol. It is also a New Testament Greek word that means "winner." *Hyper* is another Greek word. We've used it as a prefix to describe children whose activity level makes us dizzy. It means "super."

When you put *nike* and *hyper* together, you get the word that Paul made up because he could find no other word strong enough to describe who we are by faith in Jesus Christ. He said, "We are more than conquerors" (Romans 8:37). Paul defines us as super-winners, super-victors, way-above-the-rim slamdunkers. No matter what kind of worn-out old sneakers you've got on, in Christ, by grace, through faith, we have power.

This faith is never a dead thing or a passive thing. A dead faith is no faith at all. Martin Luther helps us understand what Christian faith is. Faith is "a living, energetic, active, mighty thing." Luther calls faith "daring confidence in the grace of God."[4]

We serve a living God. Living in the words of the Bible. Living in the water of Baptism. Living in the wine and bread. Jesus is the living bread. As a living thing, faith will dare to go where others fear to walk. God has not given us a spirit of fear; God has given us faith.

Faith has the same goal that Winston Churchill had in World War II. Someone once asked Churchill what his objective was for England. He replied: "You ask what is our aim? Victory at all costs. Victory in spite of all terrors. Victory, however long and hard the road may be. For without victory there is no survival."

That sounds a lot like what John was talking about when he said, "This is the victory that has overcome the world, even our faith" (1 John 5:4). Not your mother's faith or your father's faith or your pastor's faith—but the faith miraculously worked in you by the Spirit through Word and sacraments.

We know that it's easy to be full of faith when the seas are calm and the skies are sunny and the wind is at your back and the bills are paid and the children are well behaved. But when the storms of life are raging, when all signs and indicators point only to disaster, doom, and defeat, then the challenge of faith is personal.

Here comes Jesus with his answer. Here comes Jesus with his sign of victory, which is actually at first a symbol of defeat: the cross of Calvary. In the cross, we see defeat and victory wrapped up together. In the cross, we see every troubling question of life, as well as the triumphant answer—the Giver of eternal life and the Forgiver for our earthly strife. In the cross, we see the sting of death, human sin, as well as the one who took the sting away. In the cross, we see a sign with power to overcome death, the sign in which we can now conquer.

Constantine started his rise to become the sole ruler of the Roman Empire in the year 312 A.D. In that same year, Constantine and all his troops saw a sign in the noonday sky, a cross with a chi-rho symbol on top accompanied by the letters *IHS:* "In this sign, you will conquer." In the sign of the cross, we are more than conquerors through the one who loved us enough to suffer.

Too many of us are confused about our marching orders. We are enlisted to fight the good fight. We are conscripted to confess the faith. We've been drafted to declare the joy. We've not been called to run off in fear or to hide in foxholes of dread or to blindly accept other people's racist, pigeonhole designations as our destiny. There's no victory there.

God is calling today, calling us into mortal combat. This is a life and death thing. Ours is not an otherworldly, pie-in-the-sky war. Ours is spiritual warfare in this world. Through his Word, God is giving victory today.

The Bible's word for conversion does not mean an escape from anything. It doesn't imply a getaway from reality and from this real world. When the Bible talks about conversion, it means we engage this world in the name of Jesus with a converted perspective. Your eyesight is changed to spiritual insight. Now you're armed and dangerous and ready.

Prayer is not preparation; prayer is the battle. Those are our weapons. This is the Lord's battle. This is our victory. Our weapons are spiritual. Our battle attitude is spiritual. Our victory is spiritual. The battle is the Lord's, and the victory is ours forever.

This victory crushes the devil. Now we can speak the holy name of Jesus everywhere we go. As Martin Luther wrote in the *Large Catechism*, "To defy the devil, I say, we should always keep the holy name on our lips so that [the devil] may not be able to injure us as he is eager to do."[5]

This victory conquers death. Jesus Christ is our Lord; he busted down the door to death and defeat and burst back to life. Satan thought he had struck Christ dead with a demonic coup de grâce. Martin Luther again describes this cosmic battle in a stanza of an Easter hymn:

It was a strange and dreadful strife
When life and death contended;
The victory remains with life,
The reign of death was ended.
Holy Scripture plainly says
That death is swallowed up by death,
Its sting is lost forever. Alleluia![6]

Alleluia means "Praise the Lord!" We ought to raise our voices and praise him, raise our hands and praise him, thanking God for another soul snatched by Christ from the claws of hell and the jaws of the devil. That's a reason to rejoice. In Christ we have the victory, a victory more certain than any football game, a victory more solid than gold, a victory that breaks the chains of silence, a victory that will not let us stagnate or sit still. And one day we will put on some new shoes that won't ever wear out, that Jesus Christ paid for in full, and we'll dance, dance, dance, all over heaven.

Jesus paid a high price so we can win, and one day, thank

God, we'll do a touchdown end-zone dance. One day we'll join a victory parade. One day we'll sing and shout: This is the feast of victory for our God. Alleluia! Amen.

But God

ULMER MARSHALL JR.

Considered by many to be the dean of black Lutheran preachers, in his distinctive baritone, Marshall elucidates on the gracious, forgiving character of God with the King-like refrain, "But God."

God's grace, mercy, and peace be with you in the name of Jesus.

I say like the apostle Peter in his experience on the mountain top, " 'Tis good, Lord, to be here." " 'Tis good, Lord, to be here." I am glad to be in the service of the Lord one more time. I am glad … I am glad … I am glad … Ain't you glad?

Come with me, if you please, to the Word of God recorded in the book of Ephesians, the second chapter, verses one through 10. And it reads:

> *As for you, you were dead in your transgressions and sins, in which you used to live when you followed the ways of this world and of the ruler of the kingdom of the air, the spirit who is now at work in those who are disobedient. All of us also lived among them at one time, gratifying the cravings of our sinful nature and following its desires and thoughts. Like the rest, we were by nature objects of wrath. But because of his great love for us, God, who is rich in mercy, made us alive with Christ even when we were dead in transgressions—it is by grace you have been saved. And God raised us up with Christ and seated us with him in the heavenly realms in Christ Jesus, in order that in the coming ages he might show the incomparable*

riches of his grace, expressed in his kindness to us in
Christ Jesus. For it is by grace you have been saved,
through faith—and this not from yourselves, it is the
gift of God—not by works, so that no one can boast.
For we are God's workmanship, created in Christ
Jesus to do good works, which God prepared in
advance for us to do.

Paul, in his message to the Christians at Ephesus in chapter 2, paints a morbid picture of the condition of the people living there and of all mankind who enter into this world. And then he declares in verses 4 and 5: "But God, who is rich in mercy, for his great love wherewith he loved us. Even when we were dead in sins, hath quickened us together with Christ, (by grace ye are saved.)"

I want to lift up those two words, which upon surface examination may make no sense at all, but we pray that the Holy Spirit will breathe on them. Those two words are in verse 4: But God. But God.

Verses one through 10 of chapter 2 depict in typical Pauline language our old condition and the continued condition of those who don't know the Lord, those who are dead in trespasses and sin and all the consequences thereof. It is a vivid account of the state in which we find ourselves as unredeemed humanity.

The picture of lost humanity is so real: unholy conversation, giving in to the lust of the flesh, by nature children of disobedience. That is the picture painted by Paul, and the pain is terribly pronounced—helplessness and hopelessness—despair all around.

And then, with no warning at all, a note is sounded, a trumpet is lifted, there is a giving of notice concerning a glorious dawning. And it is given by way of a conjunction—the conjunction *but*. What a wonderful conjunction; and never was the conjunction *but* more graciously implored.

Paul says that deep despair and deep gloom catheterize the whole human race. Sin is everywhere and divine wrath is sure to come. And then, out of the tomb of despair, seemingly from nowhere, words spring forth that are able to change this whole ugly picture. Paul declares, *"But God,* but God."

The sin problem, says Paul, was a death problem. We were dead—born dead, dead in trespasses, dead in sins—separated from God by original sin, imputed sin, sins transmitted to all the children of Adam. Born in sin and shaped in iniquity. Sin everywhere, in everything, and in everybody. Born by nature the children of disobedience, we didn't have to learn to do wrong. No. No. We don't have to teach our children to do wrong. Just leave them alone; by nature they will do wrong. It's in them, born in them. Parents, don't be amazed at what these little ones won't do. Sin has to be unlearned, and the only way it can be unlearned is through intimacy with Christ.

Citizens for hell, unqualified for any help, no hope for tomorrow, hopelessly dead. But God. But God. But God, who is rich in mercy. Hallelujah! I am glad that we have a merciful God. Not only is he a merciful God, but Paul says he's rich in mercy. So rich in mercy that even while we were dead in sin, he has brought us to life together with Christ Jesus. Oh, what a merciful God.

What a wonderful reversal: ruined, rushing to damnation, headed for hell, captured and controlled by the terrible three—the devil, the world, and our flesh—the Prince of the Power of the air. That was our plight. But God. But God.

The reason we have to be born again is because we come here dead. We come into this world dead, spiritually dead. And no social program of any kind dreamed up by man can do away with the sin problem.

Now the experts do not use this word *sin.* They talk about crime, devious behavior, social maladjustment, antisocial behavior, and a host of other "isms." They don't like sin talk. For you see, when they call it what it really is, it forces us to deal with the God factor. But whatever tag you put on it, it's still sin. For the sin problem is everywhere. It is in the slums and the suburbs; it's in the suites as well as the streets. It's in my house and the White House; it's in the alleys and on the avenues; it's uptown as well as downtown; it's in the clubhouse as well as the church-house. It's in blacks as well as whites; wherever, whoever, whenever—the sin curse is real. And we see the evidence of it every day. It shows its ugly head in disobedience, killing, raping, dope, etc.

If you want a better understanding of what is wrong with the world, just read this passage again when you get home: Ephesians 2:1–3.

Without the "But God" reality, we make our journey under the devil's direction. We are subject to the Prince of Power of the air. But God is the turning point on the highway of life. But God is the means of a changing of direction and of a changing of destination and of a change in our living. But God allows for the switching of tracks, the moving from sin to salvation, from dead in trespasses and sin to alive in Christ Jesus.

The big evil three—the devil, the world, and our flesh—are against this switching. The world does not like saved sinners. The world hates dead folks who come alive. Don't be deceived. If you are alive in Christ, then the world hates you. But if you are still dead in sins, then you have a friend in the big three—the devil, the world, and your flesh.

There is something about this "But God" business that refuses to be silenced. I suppose it has to do with the reality of a great change, a turning around. It has to do with people who can't help talking about how they got over and what the Lord has done for them.

For you see, it is the language that declares that when nothing else could help, love lifted me. Paul declares that grace and mercy lifted him. We were dead, but God quickened us through Christ Jesus. Oh, what great love. Paul would tell you that he, too, was headed down the road to destruction, down the Damascus road, but God lifted him.

The Bible is a book complete with "But God" testimonies. Noah will tell you that the whole earth was judged and condemned, "but God in his rich mercy spared me and mine."

Abraham will tell you, "I left my home and family, not knowing where I was bound, but God led and directed me."

Moses will testify, "I didn't know how I would get that crowd out of Egypt and across the Red Sea, but God parted the waters by his power."

Daniel speaks up: "I was thrown in a den of lions, but God ... but God."

The three Hebrew boys declare together, "They cast us in a fiery furnace. But God."

I hear Ezekiel testifying, "I was led out into a valley of dry bones where I was surrounded by death. But God ... but God was able to give life to those dry dead bones."

Blind Bartemaeus wants to talk: "I have something to say. I sat by the roadside one day. They told me to be quiet. But God! He stopped to hear my humble cry."

Lazarus says, "While they are talking, I got to tell him my story. I died one day. I was buried in Bethany and in the fourth day of my decay. But God, he called my name and I had to answer."

Even the Savior will tell you: "I submitted my life to my enemies, to that wicked coalition of Jerusalem religion and Roman politics. They crucified me one Friday, and I was buried in Joseph's new tomb. They all thought I was finished. *But God.* He raised me up on the third day and gave me power both over heaven and earth."

Every believer has a "But God" testimony, and some of us have several. All of us who trust in God can give our testimonies.

I once was lost. *But God.* I was blind. *But God.* I was hell bound. *But God.* I was ignorant in my sins. *But God.*

You will be able to say, "I have had rough mountains to climb. *But God.* The way has been stormy and harsh. *But God.* I didn't see my way through many times. *But God.*"

"Once I was sick, and they said I wouldn't get well. *But God!*" You might be able to testify, "I was strung out on drugs and alcohol. But God." "My enemies and my foes came upon me to destroy me. But God." "I have known heartbreaks and heartaches. But God!"

I tell you, it's a language of intervention. He has a way of stepping in just when you need him most. It is also the language of reversal; he majors in turning things around.

Now if you came here without a "But God" testimony, you can leave here with one. Only believe in the Lord Jesus Christ and you shall be saved. When the jailer at Philippi asked Paul, "What must I do to be saved?" I hear the apostle Paul saying, "Believe, believe on the Lord Jesus Christ and you shall, oh, you shall be saved." If you believe, that will give you a "But God" testimony, and I guarantee for the rest of your life, you will keep on having them.

For he makes a difference in our lives day by day. And we ought to be willing to tell that wherever we go.

Every time Satan thought he had me down, every time he pointed the condemning finger at me, Oh, I cry out, "But God." "But God" has washed me in the blood of the Lamb. Oh, I can join in with the hymn writer, "What can wash away my sins? What can make me whole again? Nothing, nothing but the blood of Jesus." Jesus washes me clean and lifts me up and says to you and me, "You are more than conquerors in Christ Jesus."

Every time hell hounds get on my trail, every time the world tries to drag me down, every time somebody tells me I can't make it because of the color of my skin, I declare with Paul, "But God!"

When they say this can't be done or that can't be done, I declare, "But God, who is rich in mercy, has brought me through." He is able to bring you through. He is able to bring you from dead in sin to alive in Christ. He is able to bring you through the troubles of this old world. He is able to bring you from eternal death to eternal life, from hell to heaven. *But God.*

Do you know whom I am talking about? I am talking about the one true God, the triune God—Father, Son, and Holy Spirit. God!

Jesus, Remember Me!
STEPHEN A. WIGGINS SR.

This sermon was preached on Palm Sunday 1997. The preacher uses a simple plea for mercy, "Remember me!" to connect the Gospel to human needs. Based on Luke 23:26–43

I invite you now to join hands with those nearest you as we go to God in prayer.

Indeed, Lord, we are here this morning to lift you up and to thank you for being the kind of God that you are. We know it was you who woke us up this morning, and it was you who started us on our way. You gave us food to eat and clothing to wear. You even put a roof over our heads. Then, Lord, you gave us the ability to work, whether we worked or not. You gave us the ability to provide for ourselves so we might give a response to your goodness and to your mercy.

And, Lord, you've allowed us to gather here in this, your house of worship, your sanctuary. Lord, you've granted your Spirit to your people. We ask that you would clear our minds, Lord, and prepare us to receive your Word this day. Enable us to hear what you would say to us this morning so when we leave this place we'll be better people than we were when we came.

Come now, Lord, and rescue me from me. Hide me behind your cross. Let these, your people, hear your words despite anything that I might say or do. Let the words of our mouths and the meditations of our hearts be acceptable in your holy and righteous sight because you are our strength and our redeemer.

Now, Lord, let your words be powerful! Let your Spirit be with us! O God, bless your words, and bless all those who are brought aboard your ship this day. Let the whole church say, Amen, Amen, and Amen!

Read the text.

Our theme for this morning is: Jesus, remember me! Jesus remember me! Turn to your neighbor and say, "Neighbor, I shall hope: Jesus remembers me!" And neighbor, turn back and say, "I do too!"

There comes a time in each of our lives, my brothers and sisters, when it's good to know that the Lord is on our side. Sometimes we can get so sick, and we know there's nobody else who can make us well. We get backed up into some corners, and we know that there's nobody else who can pull us out of those corners. We spend our money and can't pay our bills, and we know that if it's not for the Lord looking down on us, those bills would never get paid! There are times when it's just good to know that God remembers you and that God hears you when you cry.

We have a classic example of such a time in this morning's text. It is the well-known story of the thief, or should I say, two thieves on their crosses. One accepts the Lord just in the nick of time, and the other does not. This morning, we're going to talk about the benefits of being on the Lord's side.

I want to start this morning with a question. Then there are two points that I want to make. The question is: What does it take to have Jesus remember you? What does it take to have Jesus remember you?

Now to answer that question, point number 1 is: You've got to be willing to admit that you are wrong and confess it—publicly! Let me say that again: You've got to be willing to admit you are wrong and confess it—publicly!

Some theologians debate the history of this thief on the cross. Some argue that this thief was just like the other criminal. He was insulting Jesus. He was talking about Jesus. He was teasing Jesus. Then all of a sudden the Holy Spirit fell on him and he had an instantaneous change in his personality. He turned from being evil to being good, then he called on the name of the Lord. Other theologians say that at the time that he was caught, he became repentant. Therefore, as he hung on the cross, he was already sorry for his sins and couldn't do anything else but call on the name of the Lord.

It really doesn't matter whether he came to repentance instantaneously while hanging on the cross or whether he became repentant after he had been caught. The point is that he became repentant, that he was willing to admit that he was wrong and sorry for what he had done and was being punished justly.

I like this thief on the cross! I like him because he was able to confess that he was wrong! He wasn't able to go back and change any of the things that he had done. I know there are times in my own life when I wish I could go back and change some of the things that I've done wrong. He couldn't do that, but he was able to say, "I was wrong, and I'm getting what I deserve because of what I have done"! He evidently understood what we all must understand—that for whatever we do wrong, there's always a price to pay. He was willing to pay the price. I like this thief. He didn't say to the other man, "Look what you got me into!" (You know how we do! Amen!) He didn't say that. He didn't say, "This is all your fault!" He didn't say, "If it hadn't been for you, I wouldn't be in this situation." What did he say? He said, "We are getting what we deserve, but this man, Jesus, has done nothing wrong!"

You know some of us are going to hell, blaming our circumstances on other people. It's hard, real hard, for some of us to admit that we are wrong. (Am I right about it?) Some of us blame everybody but ourselves!

I've counseled a few people in my young ministry, and sometimes one person will say openly, "The problem is not with me." Their marriage is in trouble, but they haven't done a thing wrong. They're cheating on their spouse, but their spouse drove them to do it. It wasn't their fault! They've got a drinking problem, but it was the spouse who drove them to drink. It wasn't their problem. They've got a drug problem, but it was the spouse who caused them to use. Folks can't keep a job because something's always wrong with the boss, but they've had 15 bosses. I'm not the smartest person in the world, but you mean tell me that out of 15 bosses, none of them was good? (Come on now!)

Somewhere along the way, you've got to be able to say there's a problem with me! I did something wrong. It's my fault. I deserve what has happened. I brought it on myself. It's not because God is being mean to me, it's because I'm being mean to myself! It's not because God is abusing me, it's because I'm abusing myself! If you don't admit that you've done something wrong, God can't do anything with you! There are many people running around saying that because it feels good it must be the right thing to do. No! No! No! No! No! No! (Come on, now! I know I'm right about it!) Just because something looks good to you and feels good to you doesn't necessarily make it right. (Come on, now! Am I right about it?)

I like this thief on the cross. He had robbed. He had stolen. He had killed. Now as he was faced with the reality of his crimes, he confesses that all he has done was wrong. He's saying that God is a just God! God is a good God! God is just giving me what I deserve! Then he looks over at Jesus and says, "Jesus, when you come into your kingdom, *just remember me!*" Just think about me, even though I know I don't deserve it. I know I've done some things wrong, Lord, and I deserve to be hanging here. I know I'm not even worthy to ask, Lord, but just remember me!

I like this thief. And let me tell you something else, God's people: Thank God that he does not give us what we deserve! If God were to give us what we deserve, we wouldn't have our health and our strength, we wouldn't have food on our tables and clothes on our backs, we wouldn't have a roof over our heads. If God were to give us what we deserve, we wouldn't have jobs, we wouldn't have eyes to see, we wouldn't have legs to walk, we wouldn't have ears to hear, we wouldn't have tongues to speak. If God were to give us what we deserve, most of us, if not all of us, would be dead and gone! We wouldn't have a home, we wouldn't have a job, we wouldn't have any money. Talk about being broke, you'd be broke!

Thank God that he doesn't give us what we deserve! But when we call on him, when we confess our faults, when we say, "Lord, I know I haven't served you like I should. I know I haven't done the things that you've required of me. I know I haven't been faithful in my giving. I know I haven't loved my brothers and sisters like you told me to. I know I haven't forgiven others as you have forgiven me, but I need you, Lord. I'm calling on you, Lord, right now! And he saves us! He forgives us! He remembers that he loves us always and wants us to call on him.

And that brings me to point number 2. Point number 2 is: You've got to ask the Lord for help! (Lord, remember me!) In chapter 38, Isaiah tells King Hezekiah, "Hezekiah, get your house in order, for today, you shall surely die." And Hezekiah doesn't do anything special, he just falls on his knees and says, "Lord, oh Lord, don't you remember, Lord? Don't you remember that I prayed? Don't you remember that I was just? Don't you remember that I was faithful? Don't you remember that I was righteous? Don't you remember that I was on your side, Lord?"

And before Isaiah could get down the street, the Lord called Isaiah and said to go back and tell King Hezekiah, "I have remembered! Tell him that I have remembered his prayers. I have remembered his faithfulness. I have remembered his justness. I have remembered his righteousness. You tell Hezekiah that he has 15 more years!"

I know what you're thinking. You're saying, "Well, Pastor Wiggins, that was way back in Bible times, and maybe God is acting differently now!" Is it all right if I talk to you this morning? Can I tell you something? I don't know about you, but I've been in some situations that nobody but the Lord Jesus Christ could get me out of. Let me share my testimony with you this morning.

I remember when I was about 8 or 9 years old. My father put a hoe in my hands to work in the fields. (Some of you know something about that. All of you didn't grow up in the city!). But I remember this one Saturday afternoon. We had worked all morning and my mother had taken us to the swimming pool to have a little fun and relaxation. I remember as we would go down there, there would always be a young boy about 15 or 16 years old there by the name of Jeffrey Moore. I remember saying to myself, "Jeffrey must have grown up in the water because he can swim like a fish." I didn't like Jeffrey because he would show off all the time. He was a great swimmer, and all I could do was dog paddle. (Some of you know what I'm talking about!)

One afternoon while I was trying to be more than I could be,

I walked down the side of the pool. I had measured where it was just deep enough where I could jump in and when I came up I could stand. That afternoon my measurements came up short. When I jumped in and came up, I went right back down again. Right away I knew I was in trouble, but I didn't have sense enough to start calling for help.

Fear began to take over my body. I went down a second time and came back up. This time there was just one thing on my mind. There was just one thing left that I wanted to say. It wasn't sophisticated. It wasn't educated. I just wanted to call out with my last breath, "Help!" But I didn't have time to do that because I was already on my way back down.

But all of a sudden I felt two hands grab me, one on each side of my waist. They lifted me up until I felt my head break through the top of the water. I didn't stop moving until I was at the side of the pool. Before I could say anything or turn around to see who it was, I heard the familiar voice of Jeffrey Moore. He said to me, "You're gonna be all right now!"

And people, I just laid there with tears running down my face because I knew what I had thought about him. I knew that if it had been up to me, Jeffrey wouldn't have even been in that pool. And I knew then what it meant to have the Lord looking down on you and looking out for you and remembering that you're one of his children! Remembering that you tried to be faithful. Remembering that you tried to do what's right!

And even though Jeffrey didn't know what I thought about him, he jumped in and saved me. Even though I didn't deserve it! And it wasn't Jeffrey's fault that I was being stupid! It wasn't his fault!

Let me tell you something, God's People, it's not Jesus' fault when we act stupid. It's not his fault! It's not Jesus' fault when we do something wrong. It's not Jesus' fault when we steal and get caught. It's not Jesus' fault when we swear and curse and lie! That's not his fault! It's not his fault when we get caught cheating on our spouses. It's not his fault when we spend all our money and we can't pay our bills. That's not Jesus' fault! It's not his fault when we turn our backs on God time and time again. It's not his fault when we do stupid things and end up sick and no one can make us well. That's not Jesus' fault! That's our fault!

But thank God that for some reason, and I don't know why, Jesus looks beyond our faults and sees our needs! And I don't know why Jesus loves us like he does. I don't know why he cares for us the way that he does! I don't know why he sacrificed his life the way that he did! But I'm so glad. I don't know about you, but I'm so glad that he did!

You know even now, when things aren't going just right, the Lord has already done so much for me that I don't ask him for much these days. I just ask him to remember me. I've done some things wrong Lord, but, Jesus, remember me. I haven't always been on your side, Lord, but, Jesus, remember me. I'm not asking to sit on your right side or your left side, I just want you to remember me. I'm not asking for a chair beside your throne, Jesus, just remember me. I don't need a place of distinction like Abraham, I just want to be remembered! I don't need a long white robe or a golden crown or even silver slippers, Jesus, just remember me. I don't need a trumpet like Gabriel. I don't need a ladder like Jacob. I don't need an ark like Noah. I don't need to see a wheel in the middle of a wheel like Ezekiel.

Lord Jesus, just remember me!

I just need you to remember me. Just think about me, Lord. Just remember that I am yours, Lord Jesus! Because you told me that you were going to prepare a place for me and that you would come back and get me so that wherever you are, there I might be also! Thank you, Jesus. Thank you, Lord! Thank you for remembering.

God's people, go in the knowledge that God hears your prayers. Know that God answers your prayers. Know that God is always on your side!

To him alone we give the glory, the honor, and the praise! Amen, Amen, and Amen!

Notes

All interviews were conducted in person or via telephone by John A. Nunes in March 1996. Our thanks to those who gave of their time to be part of this project.

Introduction

1 Joyce Carol Oates, "A Lost Generation," review of *Cold New World: Growing Up in a Harder Country,* by William Finnegan, *New York Times Book Review,* 16 July 1998, 12.

Chapter 1: What Is Urban?

1 Karl Barth, *Homiletics,* trans. Geoffrey W. Bromiley and Donald E. Daniels, (Louisville: Westminster John Knox Press, 1991), 17.

2 Theodore G. Tappert, ed., *The Book of Concord* (Philadelphia: Fortress Press, 1983), 112.

Chapter 2: Making All Things New

1 Marilyn J. Harran, *Martin Luther: Learning for Life* (St. Louis: Concordia, 1997). See particularly chapter 5, "Martin Luther: '*Docendi sunt christiani.*' "

2 Martin H. Franzmann, *The Word of the Lord Grows* (St. Louis: Concordia, 1961), 54.

3 Tappert, 304.

4 Martin Luther King Jr., *Where Do We Go from Here: Chaos or Community?* (New York: Harper and Row, 1967).

5 C. S. Lewis, *Letters to Malcolm: Chiefly on Prayer* (New York: Harcourt Brace, 1983).

6 Stanley M. Hauerwas, *Wilderness Wanderings: Probing Twentieth-Century Theology and Philosophy* (New York: HarperCollins; Boulder, Colo.: Westview Press, 1997), 122.

7 Tappert, 391.

8 H. George Anderson, convocation presentation at Concordia Seminary, St. Louis, Mo., 3 February 1998.

9 C. Eric Lincoln and Lawrence H. Mamiya, *The Black Church in The African American Experience* (Durham: Duke University Press, 1990).

10 Nicholas Lemann, "The Myth of Community Development," *New York Times Magazine*, 9 January 1994, page. Reprinted by permission of International Creative Management, Inc. Copyright ©1994 Nicholas Lemann.

11 Thomas Sowell, *Is Reality Optional? And Other Essays* (Stanford, Calif.: Hoover Institution Press, 1993), 89.

Chapter 3: Dangerous Disconnections

1 Tappert, 412.

2 Gerhard O. Forde, *Justification by Faith: A Matter of Death and Life* (Ramsey, N.J.: Sigler Press, 1990), 93.

3 Peter Steinke, "Beliefs: Speculating on Wars of the Future: Instead of Ideologies, the Combatants May Be Cultures," *New York Times*, 16 April 1994.

4 Paul R. Raabe, "Christ and American Culture: Some Biblical Reflections," *Christ and Culture: The Church in a Post-Christian? America*, Concordia Seminary

Monograph Series, Symposium Papers, 4 (St. Louis, 1995). The quote in the second bulleted point is from page 37.

5 Thomas Sowell, *Migrations and Cultures: A World View* (New York: BasicBooks, HarperCollins, 1996). See especially the section on "Cultural Capital," 379–383.

6 Nathan Mitchell, "Cult, Creed, and Culture," *Liturgy Digest* 3, no 2 (1996), 47. Reprinted with permission of Notre Dame Center for Pastoral Liturgy.

7 Tappert, 32.

8 Ibid, 32.

9 Extract from *God in the Dock* by C. S. Lewis copyright ©1970 by C. S. Lewis Pte. Ltd., reproduced by permission of Curtis Brown, London. 98.

10 Ibid.

11 Stanley Hauerwas, "Preaching as though We Had Enemies," *First Things* 53 (May 1995), 46.

Chapter 4: Clashing of Kingdoms

1 Ethan Bronner, "Inventing the Notion of Race: Some Scholars Say the Label Evolved Recently as a Tool of the Vanquished as Well as the Victors," *New York Times,* 10 January 1998, A15.

2 David H. Behnke, "Multicultural Worship: Urban LCMS Mission Perspectives," *Lutheran Worship Notes* 31, 1.

3 Dinesh D'Souza, *The End of Racism: Principles for a Multiracial Society* (New York: The Free Press, 1995), 486.

4 Tappert, 310.

Chapter 5: Tumbling Walls

1 Tappert, 31.

2 Samuel Johnson, "London: A Poem"

3 Tappert, 389.

4 Martin Luther King Jr., "A Christmas Sermon on Peace," *A Testament of Hope* (New York: Harper & Row, 1986).

5 "There is a Balm in Gilead." The Commission on Worship of The Lutheran Church—Missouri Synod, *Hymnal Supplement 98* (St. Louis: Concordia, 1998), 889.

6 Paul Laurence Dunbar, "Sympathy." Included in *The Poetry of the Negro 1746–1970,* edited by Langston Hughes and Anna Bontemps (New York: Doubleday Anchor).

Chapter 6: Just Words

1 Rudolph H. Blank, "Six Theses Concerning Freedom in Christ and Liberation," *Concordia Journal* 20, no. 3 (July 1994), 239.

2 J.A.O. Preus III, New Horizons presentation at Concordia Publishing House (1997). Preus offered a critical analysis of how metaphors function in language, especially in relation to the doctrine of justification. A book on this subject is forthcoming from Concordia.

3 Robert Kolb, *Speaking the Gospel Today: A Theology of Evangelism,* rev. ed., (St. Louis: Concordia, 1995), 169.

Chapter 7: Countering Counterfeit Liberation

1 Jürgen Moltmann, *The Crucified God: The Cross of Christ as the Foundation and Criticism of Christian Theology* (New York: Harper and Row, 1974), 329. Used with permission of HarperCollins Publishers Inc.

2 Cornel West, *Prophesy Deliverance! An Afro-American Revolutionary Christianity* (Philadelphia: The Westminster Press, 1982), 99–126.

3 James H. Harris, *Pastoral Theology: A Black-Church Perspective* (Minneapolis: Fortress Press, 1991), 56.

4 Martin H. Franzmann, "O God, O Lord of Heaven and Earth," Copyright ©1967 Lutheran Council in the USA. Reprinted by permission of Augsburg Fortress.

5 Shelby Steele, *The Content of Our Character: A New Vision of Race in America* (New York: St. Martin's Press, 1990). This theme is woven throughout the volume.

6 Gerhard Aho, "Law and Gospel in Preaching," *Concordia Theological Quarterly* 45, no. 1–2 (1981), 3. Appendix III in Richard R. Caemmerer's *Preaching for the Church* (St. Louis: Concordia, 1959) is devoted to "Biblical Modes of Depicting the Atonement."

7 Ross Aden, "Justification and Sanctification: A Conversation between Lutheranism and Orthodoxy," *St. Vladimir's Theological Quarterly* 38, no. 1 (1994).

8 Joseph Sittler, *The Ecology of Faith: The New Situation in Preaching* (Philadelphia: Fortress Press, 1961), 36.

9 Aden, 92–93. Used by permission of *St. Vladimir's Theological Quarterly*, 575 Scarsdale Rd., Crestwood, NY, 10707.

10 Robert D. Preus, "Perennial Problems in the Doctrine of Justification," *Concordia Theological Quarterly* 45, no. 3 (1981), 169.

11 Robert W. Jenson, "The 'Sorry' State of Lutherans," *dialog* 22 (Fall 1983), 281.

12 Steele, 77–92.

13 Ibid, 49.

14 Andrew Weyermann, "The Gospel and Life in Preaching," *Concordia Theological Monthly* XL, no. 6–7 (1969), 125 (445).

15 Charles T. Shannon, " 'An Ante-bellum Sermon': A Resource for an African-American Hermeneutic" in *Stony the Road We Trod: African American Biblical Interpretation,* ed. Cain Hope Felder (Minneapolis: Fortress Press, 1991), 122.

16 Steele, 108.

17 Herman G. Stuempfle Jr., *Preaching Law and Gospel* (Philadelphia: Fortress Press, 1978), 49.

18 Jaroslav Pelikan, *Jesus through the Centuries: His Place in the History of Culture* (New Haven: Yale University Press, 1985), 100.

19 Etienne Charpentier, *How to Read the New Testament,* trans. John Bowden (New York: Crossroad, 1982), 18.

20 "Lo, Judah's Lion Wins the Strife," *Lutheran Worship* (St. Louis: Concordia, 1982), 146.

21 Ronald Feuerhahn, foreword to *Ha! Ha! Among the Trumpets: Sermons by Martin H. Franzmann* (St. Louis: Concordia, 1994).

22 Henry H. Mitchell, *Celebration and Experience in Preaching* (Nashville: Abingdon Press, 1990), 65–66. Copyright ©1990 by Abingdon Press. Used by permission.

23 Tappert, 126.

Chapter 8: Saying It in the City

1 Lowell C. Green, unpublished Lutheran Pastors Study Group, Bethany Lutheran Church, Buffalo, New York, (2 December 1992).

Chapter 9: Three Voices from the City

1 Alan L. Keyes, *Masters of the Dream: The Strength and Betrayal of Black America* (New York: Morrow, 1995), 15–16.

2 Richard John Neuhaus, "While We're at It," *First Things* 66 (October 1996), 87.

3 Henry Louis Gates Jr., *Loose Canons: Notes on the Culture Wars* (New York: Oxford University Press, 1992), 127.

4 Ewald Pless, *What Luther Says: A Practical In-Home Anthology for the Active Christian* (St. Louis: Concordia, 1959), 498–499.

5 Tappert, 374.

6 "Christ Jesus Lay in Death's Strong Bands," *Lutheran Worship* (St. Louis: Concordia, 1982), 123.

Bibliography

Aden, Ross. "Justification and Sanctification: A Conversation between Lutheranism and Orthodoxy." *St. Vladimir's Theological Quarterly* 38 no. 1 (1994).

Aho, Gerhard. "Law and Gospel in Preaching." *Concordia Theological Quarterly* 45, no. 1–2 (1981).

Aulén, Gustaf. *Christus Victor: An Historical Study of the Three Main Types of the Idea of Atonement.* Translated by A. G. Hebert. New York: Macmillan, 1969.

Barentsen, Jack. "The Validity of Human Language: A Vehicle for Divine Truth." *Grace Theological Journal* 9, no. 1 (1988).

Barth, Karl. *Homiletics.* Translated by Geoffrey W. Bromiley and Donald E. Daniels. Louisville: Westminster John Knox Press, 1991.

Bayliss, John F., ed., *Black Slave Narratives.* New York: Macmillan, 1970.

Behnke, David H. "Multicultural Worship: Urban LCMS Mission Perspectives." *Lutheran Worship Notes* 31 (1994).

Bennett, William J. "Revolt Against God: America's Spiritual Despair." *Policy Review* 67 (Winter 1994).

Bonhoeffer, Dietrich. *Act and Being*. Trans. Bernard Noble. New York: Harper and Row, 1961.

Buttrick, David. *A Captive Voice: The Liberation of Preaching*. Louisville: Westminster John Knox Press, 1994.

Caemmerer, Richard R. *Preaching for the Church*. St. Louis: Concordia, 1959.

Charpentier, Etienne. *How to Read the New Testament*. Translated by John Bowden. New York: Crossroad, 1982.

Christenson, Larry, ed., *Welcome, Holy Spirit: A Study of Charismatic Renewal in the Church*. Minneapolis: Augsburg, 1987.

Chupungco, Anscar J. *Cultural Adaptation of the Liturgy*. New York: Paulist Press, 1982.

Cone, James H. *My Soul Looks Back*. Nashville: Abingdon Press, 1982.

D'Souza, Dinesh. *The End of Racism: Principles for a Multiracial Society*. New York: The Free Press, 1995.

Dix, Gregory. *The Shape of the Liturgy*. New York: Seabury, 1982.

Doyle, G. Wright. "Augustine's Sermonic Method." *The Westminster Theological Journal* (Spring 1977).

DuBois, W. E. B. *The Souls of Black Folk*. New York: Bantam Classics, 1989.

Featherstone, Rudolph R. "The Theology of the Cross: The Perspective of an African in America." In *Theology and the Black Experience*, edited by Albert Pero and Ambrose Moyo. Minneapolis: Augsburg, 1988.

Feuerhahn, Ronald. Foreword to *Ha! Ha! Among the Trumpets: Sermons by Martin H. Franzmann*.

St. Louis: Concordia, 1994.

Gates, Henry Louis Jr. *Loose Canons: Notes on the Culture Wars.* New York: Oxford, 1992.

George, Nelson. *Buppies, B-Boys; Baps and Bohos: Notes on Post-Soul Black Culture.* New York: HarperCollins, 1992.

Green, Lowell C. Unpublished Lutheran Pastors Study Group. Bethany Lutheran Church, Buffalo, New York. 2 December 1992.

Gutierrez, Gustavo. "The Hope of Liberation." In *Mission Trends No.3: Third World Theologies,* edited by Gerald H. Anderson and Thomas F. Stransky. New York: Paulist Press; Grand Rapids: Eerdmans, 1976.

Harris, James H. *Pastoral Theology: A Black-Church Perspective.* Minneapolis: Fortress Press, 1991.

Hauerwas, Stanley. "Preaching as though We Had Enemies." *First Things* 53 (May 1995).

Hauerwas, Stanley and William H. Willimon. *Resident Aliens: Life in the Christian Colony.* Nashville: Abingdon Press, 1989.

Hesselgrave, David J. *Communicating Christ Cross-Culturally: An Introduction to Missionary Communication.* Grand Rapids: Zondervan, 1991.

Jenson, Robert W. "The 'Sorry' State of Lutherans." *dialog* 22 (Fall 1983).

Johnson, John Franklin. "Hermeneutics in Thomas Aquinas: An Appraisal and Appreciation." *Concordia Theological Quarterly* 45, no. 3 (July 1981).

Kelly, John Norman Davidson. *Early Christian Doctrines.* New York: Harper and Row, 1960.

Kesich, Veselin. "The Orthodox Church and Biblical Interpretation." *St. Vladimir's Theological Quarterly* 37, no. 4 (1993).

Keyes, Alan L. *Masters of the Dream: The Strength and Betrayal of Black America*. New York: Morrow, 1995.

King, Martin Luther Jr. "A Christmas Sermon on Peace." In *A Testament of Hope*. New York: Harper & Row, 1986.

Koester, Helmut. *History and Literature of Early Christianity*. Vol. 2 of *Introduction to the New Testament*. Philadelphia: Fortress, 1983.

Kraft, Charles H. *Christianity in Culture: A Study in Dynamic Biblical Theologizing in Cross-Cultural Perspective*. Maryknoll: Orbis Books, 1979.

Lathrop, Gordon W. "Baptism in the New Testament and Its Cultural Settings." In *Worship and Culture in Dialogue*. Geneva: Lutheran World Federation, 1994.

Lincoln, C. Eric, and Lawrence H. Mamiya. *The Black Church in the African American Experience*. Durham: Duke University Press, 1990.

Lischer, Richard. "Recent Books on Preaching." *Word and World* 7, no. 1 (Winter 1987).

Lundin, Roger. *The Culture of Interpretation: Christian Faith and the Postmodern World*. Grand Rapids: Eerdmans, 1993.

Mitchell, Henry H. *Black Preaching: The Recovery of a Powerful Art*. Nashville: Abingdon Press, 1990.

———. *Celebration and Experience in Preaching*. Nashville: Abingdon Press, 1990.

Mitchell, Nathan. "Cult, Creed, and Culture." *Liturgy Digest* 3, no. 2 (1996).

Moellering, H. Armin. "Timeo Praedicaturus." *Concordia Journal* 8, no. 3 (May 1982).

Morris, Leon. *The Apostolic Preaching of the Cross*. Grand Rapids: Eerdmans, 1965.

Moyd, Olin P. *The Sacred Art: Preaching and Theology in the African American Tradition.* Valley Forge: Judson Press, 1995.

Murphy, Joseph M. *Working the Spirit: Ceremonies of the African Diaspora.* Boston: Beacon, 1994.

Neuhaus, Richard John. "The Longest War." *First Things* 47 (November 1994).

Oleska, Michael. " 'The Gospel and Culture' at the National Workshop on Christian Unity." *Saint Vladimir's Theological Quarterly* 36, no. 4 (1992).

Owens, James Garfield. *All God's Chillun: Meditations on Negro Spirituals.* Nashville: Abingdon Press, 1971.

Page, Clarence. "Will African American Be the Next Ethnic Term in Our Lexicon?" *Buffalo News* (2 January 1989).

Pero, Albert. "On Being Black, Lutheran, and American in a Racist Society." In *Theology and the Black Experience,* edited by Albert Pero and Ambrose Moyo. Minneapolis: Augsburg, 1988.

Petterson, Eugene H. "Introduction to the New Testament." In *The Message.* Colorado Springs: NavPress Publishing Group, 1995.

Pfitzner, V. C. "The Hermeneutical Problem and Preaching." *Concordia Theological Monthly* 38, no. 6 (June 1967).

Pollard, Leslie N. "Saga and Song: A Cross-cultural Primer in African-American Preaching." *Ministry* 68, no. 5 (May 1995).

Reagles, Steven L. "Preaching the Imprint of Paradox." *Concordia Journal* 11, no. 5 (September 1985).

Roberts, Sam. "Conversations/Kenneth B. Clark: An Integrationist to This Day, Believing All Else Has Failed." *New York Times* (7 May 1995).

Robinson, Beverly. "Historical Arenas of African American Storytelling." In *Talk That Talk: An Anthology of African American Storytelling*, edited by Linda Goss and Marian E. Barnes. New York: Touchstone Simon & Schuster, 1989.

Rossow, Francis C. Review of *Hermeneutics for Preaching: Approaches to Contemporary Interpretations of Scripture*, edited by Raymond Bailey. *Concordia Journal* 20, no. 2 (April 1994).

Schaibley, Robert W. "Lutheran Preaching: Proclamation, Not Communication." *Concordia Journal* 18, no. 1 (January 1992).

Scudieri, Robert J. *The Apostolic Church: One, Holy, Catholic and Missionary*. Fullerton, Calif.: Lutheran Society for Missiology, 1995.

Sittler, Joseph. *Essays on Nature and Grace*. Philadelphia: Fortress Press, 1972.

———. *The Ecology of Faith: The New Situation in Preaching*. Philadelphia: Fortress Press, 1961.

Skinner, Tom. *How Black Is the Gospel*. Philadelphia: Lippincott, 1970.

Sobrino, Jon. *The Principle of Mercy: Taking the Crucified People from the Cross*. Maryknoll: Orbis Books, 1994.

Spencer, Jon Michael. *Black Hymnody: A Hymnological History of the African-American Church*. Knoxville: University of Tennessee Press, 1992.

———. *The Emergency of Black and the Emergence of Rap*. A special issue of *Black Sacred Music* 5, no. 1 (Spring 1991). Durham: Duke University Press, 1991.

———. *Protest and Praise: Sacred Music of Black Religion*. Minneapolis: Fortress Press, 1990.

Steele, Shelby. *The Content of Our Character: A New Vision of Race in America*. New York: St. Martin's Press, 1990.

Steinke, Peter. "Beliefs: Speculating on Wars of the Future: Instead of Ideologies, the Combatants May Be Cultures." *New York Times* (16 April 1994).

Stewart, Warren H. Jr. *Interpreting God's Word in Black Preaching*. Valley Forge: Judson Press, 1984.

Stone, Robert. "The Sins of the Fathers." *New York Review of Books* (2 November 1995).

Stuempfle, Herman G. Jr. *Preaching Law and Gospel*. Philadelphia: Fortress Press, 1978.

Tappert, Theodore G., trans. and ed. *The Book of Concord: The Confessions of the Evangelical Lutheran Church*. Philadelphia: Fortress Press, 1983.

Vogel, Larry M. "Mission across Cultures and Traditional Lutheran Cultus." *Concordia Journal* vol (May 1986).

Weyermann, Andrew. "The Gospel and Life in Preaching." *Concordia Theological Monthly* XL, no. 6–7 (1969).

Willimon, William H. *Peculiar Speech: Preaching to the Baptized*. Grand Rapids: Eerdmans, 1992.

Wilmore, Gayraud S. *Black Religion and Black Radicalism*. Maryknoll: Orbis Books, 1998.

Wilson, Paul Scott. *The Practice of Preaching*. Nashville: Abingdon Press, 1995.

Zaleski, Carol. "Joyful Witnessing: How the Descendents of Slaves Adapted to Christendom." Review of *Working the Spirit: Ceremonies of the African Diaspora,* by Joseph M. Murphy. *New York Times Book Review* (16 January 1994).